MW01681109

How to Eat Like a Hot Chick

Jodi Lipper
&
Cerina Vincent

Heyday Productions

New York Los Angeles

How to Eat Like a Hot Chick

Please visit our website:
www.heydayproductions.com

First edition published 2007
Printed in Canada

ISBN: 978-1-4243-3653-1

10 9 8 7 6 5 4 3 2 1

p.s. This book is obviously not meant to replace the care or advice of a medical professional. We think that you should always consult with a real doctor before making any radical changes to your eating habits. Please take care of yourselves! We are not responsible if you take us too seriously and get yourself sick. And if you're under 18, ask your mom if you should be reading this!

For Sherie Beth Weinstein and Nonnie,
who inspired so much of this book with their passions for food,
laughter, laughing about food, and life.

HOW TO EAT LIKE A HOT CHICK

Contents

****Hot Chick (definition):** A confident woman. She knows what she wants and gets it. She is aware of her flaws, but she doesn't obsess over them and instead thinks that maybe (just maybe) they actually add to her unique beauty. She is passionate. She loves life. She is comfortable in her own skin and owns her sexuality, but uses it purely for good. She does not see other women as her enemy and competes only with herself to do her best at all times and to be her best at all times. She is forthright, honest, disarmingly herself and tries to be no one else. She is having fun and she is sexy and you just want to be around her to soak up some of those good vibes. She isn't perfect, but she doesn't care because she is hot. And so are you.

Introduction
What Is A Hot Chick And How Can I Be One Of Those?

Welcome to the world of Hot Chicks. Guess what? You're hot! You probably didn't know that, did you? You probably think you're OKAY, but spend lots of days feeling fat and gross and LSE* as all hell. We know because we used to be like you. We used to spend lots of time obsessing about every calorie we swallowed, thinking that if we made one bad food choice we would somehow instantaneously become fat and undesirable. We woke up one day, though, and realized that the problem had nothing to do with a little too much chocolate one night or an extra slice of pizza at lunch. It was actually living in fear like this that was keeping us from really being hot.

We were wasting our heyday* by being LSE* and acting like total losers, and it was actually turning us into losers! Yikes! So we told ourselves and the universe* that we were hot and decided to just go ahead and start living like the Hot Chicks that we wanted to be. And it worked! As we started to believe that we were hot, other people started thinking we were hot, too, which made us want to take care of our bods so that we'd feel even hotter! We also started feeling more heydayish* too, which was an extra awesome benefit of eating and treating ourselves well.

Along the way, we learned exactly what foods made us feel great about ourselves, and which ones left us feeling bloated, grumpy and unsatisfied. We also learned how to prioritize which foods we didn't miss at all when we left them on our plates, and which ones were way too much fun to ever dream of giving up. We're not perfect. We fuck up* from time to time with everything from our food to our hair to our boyfriend, but we figure that it's our heyday*, so it's okay to mess up once in a while. Plus, it's so much easier to laugh at yourself and keep on chugging when you really believe that you are hot, and we want to help you realize that you are, too!

Keep in mind, when we say "hot," we are not talking about looking like you walked off the cover of a magazine, and this has absolutely nothing to do with Paris Hilton! (Just a reminder: the word "hot" was used for years before she was even legal.) Here's the secret, ladies - it's not how skinny or buff or booby you are that makes you hot, and it's not *really* what you eat, either. So why'd we write this book? Because we know that as women so much of our self esteem centers around food. What we eat has a giant effect on how we feel about ourselves, and this book will teach you what to eat to make yourself feel better and less LSE* than you ever have before.

The first step to being a Hot Chick is to get rid of all your LSE*, embrace your heyday*, and decide that you deserve all the goodness that the universe* has to offer. When we talk about Hot Chicks we are talking about those cool, confident women you see every now and then who, no matter what size they are, just ooze sex appeal and awesomeness. They always seem like they are having fun. They can confidently order a beer and a giant piece of chocolate cake, eat it alone, and then turn all the heads in the room when they walk away. These are

Hot Chicks. Hot Chicks are confident, smart, fun, kind, and never apologize for who they are, what they look like.....or what they eat.

We are so excited to share our Hot Chicks tricks to with you! WE know that you're already hot and that you have the potential to be and feel even hotter. And we promise that when you start eating like a Hot Chick, you will be loving life and having a hotter heyday* than you ever thought you could. Remember, the only thing stopping you from being hot is not knowing that you are. And you are! We promise.

Calorie Crap

We strongly believe that Hot Chicks should not obsess over every little thing that we put into our mouths (unless it's attached to a gross guy we never should have hooked up with). However, it is imperative that we all understand how many calories we need to keep us feeling hot and how many calories will only make us feel like comatose, lethargic little oinkers. (Or more accurately, big oinkers.) Now, there is some math involved here, so strap on your thinking caps and pay attention.

You've all seen the FDA's food pyramid thingy that is based on a 2,000 calorie diet. But brace yourselves, ladies, because it's total bullshit. The sad truth is, eating 2,000 calories a day is fine if you have a penis, run marathons, chop wood, work construction and/or are an aerobics instructor. But for the normal Hot Chick, 2,000 calories is too many. Now, some girls have super-duper metabolisms that keep them slim no matter how many calories they consume, but those girls are probably not reading this book. The rest of us actually have to work pretty damn hard to feel and look our best, and that includes being aware of our calories.

Most of us Hot Chicks that are between 5' and 5'9 need somewhere from 1,200 and 1,800 calories a day, depending on our activity levels. And we're not *at all* telling you to count every single morsel, but to just be smart! With the GIANT portions that restaurants serve, it is way too easy to consume 1,000 calories on a 30 minute lunch break instead of throughout the entire day. And if you had a 500 calorie bagel with cream cheese at breakfast, that's 1,500 calories before 2:00 p.m. Holy shit! And if you do this every day, we can almost guarantee that you are not feeling your hottest right now. But we can change that!

You can ignore this part completely if you want, but we thought we'd share how we break down this calorie crap. We eat a 300-400 calorie breakfast, a 400-500 calorie lunch, a 400-500 calorie dinner, and then maybe a 150 calorie snack and/or a 150 calorie alcoholic beverage at the end of a long, hard day. This keeps our metabolisms running smooth and consistently and stops us from feeling deprived or developing a giant case of OWL Syndrome*, which in turn prevents us from fucking up* and scarfing down a giant Cinnabon before catching the train home.

And please don't worry that by going against the FDA you're gonna end up malnourished and looking like you pulled a Mary Kate*. Keep in mind that the D in FDA stands for DRUG! We think that means that if you follow their rules, you're bound to end up on a bunch of drugs for fucked up* diseases like diabetes and high cholesterol, but we'll save the rest of that lecture for another book.

We also have to tell you that we keep pretty damn active in order to feel our hottest. We do some form of cardio exercise pretty much every day - yoga, running, stationary bike, butt class*, sex, etc. Now this doesn't mean that we don't totally pig out every now and then, because we TOTALLY do! Never forget that it's your heyday* and it's important to have fun!

The first rule of eating like a Hot Chick is, "chocolate cake for breakfast and a pound of spinach for dinner." That's not just to add some nutrients to our day, but it is also to balance our calorie consumption. If we eat a brunch that is well over 1,500 calories, we'll try to eat a dinner that is much, much lower in calories. This is what makes us feel better mentally and physically. It's our way of being able to enjoy the calorie-rich foods we love, have energy to do everything we want, and still feel hot in our magic* jeans. We know that the FDA can't promise you that!

Chapter 1
How to Eat Like a Hot Chick
At Breakfast

They say breakfast is the most important meal of the day, and they ain't lying. It totally sets the tone for what the rest of your day will be like. If you eat something healthy, you'll feel totally hot, and you'll want to continue putting good, nutritious food into your body all day long. But if you start on the wrong note, it's basically all downhill from there. It's easy to say, "Ah, screw it. I already fucked up* and now this day's shot. I'll just pig out for the next 12 hours and start over tomorrow."

Be aware that we girls become especially tempted to eat something really fucked up* for breakfast after a night of drinking. Alcohol lowers our blood sugar and dehydrates us, and we wake up the next morning starving and desperate for chocolate. At least WE do. You might crave pizza or some other cheesy nonsense, but that's really no better.

Yes, we firmly believe that there are some circumstances when it's okay to eat something retarded in the morning, but we'll get to those special occasions later. On a regular, average Tuesday, it is much hotter to eat something healthy. You don't want to go too far to this extreme either, though, and eat a miniscule, unsatisfying breakfast. No grape nuts. No tiny cup of yogurt. This will only lead to a major pig out the minute the office pastry tray comes out, or when you pass your first vending machine of the day, and that is exactly what we're trying to avoid.

There IS a happy medium, ladies, and we'll help you find it with these Hot Chick's tips to starting your day the best way you possibly can.

Oatmeal

One of the breakfasts we've had the most success with is good, old-fashioned oatmeal. Wait; before you make that face, hold on. We know that plain oatmeal can be boring. You've gotta jazz it up a little, and we've found some good ways to do it. Always add the little dash of salt they recommend. We also like to add cinnamon and a little bit of sugar if we're in the mood for a sweet breakfast.

If we feel like being even more virtuous, we add some chopped nuts and ground flaxseeds instead. If this sounds gross, give it a chance before you make that face again, dammit! It may take a few times to get comfortable with it (kind of like a bikini wax), but we think it's just as addictive.

We promise this stuff tastes good, but if you don't like it, that's fine. Be creative and work it out yourself. You can put fruit in your oatmeal, or anything else that sounds good to you. We have a friend that used to eat oatmeal with hummus in it. Now, that sounds pretty fucked up* and weird to us, but who are we to judge? If that sounds good to you, go for it.

The only kinds of oatmeal that we're totally going to forbid are those gross little packets of pre-flavored junk. Pay attention – it takes exactly the same amount of time to pour oatmeal into your bowl from the box as it does to open one of those stupid packets. And those packages are filled with sugar, artificial flavors, colors, preservatives, and all that bad stuff.

Plus, one of those tiny containers has the same amount of calories as a giant bowl of plain oatmeal, is far less filling, and is full of disgusting little dehydrated, shrunken peach chunks. Does that sound hot to you? And don't you dare fall for those new packages of "Women's Oatmeal." That is total bullshit and insulting to your hot little mind. There is nothing in our womanly bodies that makes us need extra artificial flavorings. Please top your oatmeal off yourselves, ladies, and you'll be much better off.

Eggs

For many years we refused to eat eggs. The whole idea of ingesting dead baby chicken fetuses just totally grossed us out. But after a while we realized that we were missing out on a ton of protein (and the great majority of breakfast options) by shunning away from the incredible edible egg. And we soon found that as long as you don't think about exactly what it is that you're eating, they're actually pretty damn good. (Isn't that true of most foods?)

If cholesterol is a big concern for you, then you should probably skip the eggs entirely, but if you're not worried about it, eggs are actually pretty cool. They have less than 100 calories each, around 7 grams of butt-muscle-building protein, and they supposedly make your brain sharper. Well, we sure think that smart girls are hot, so don't let some other bitch beat you on her IQ test just because she ate a better breakfast than you!

There are of course many ways to cook eggs - they're about as versatile as your favorite pair of magic jeans*. You can dress them up or dress them down, and they'll pretty much always make you happy. However, there are also many, many ways to fuck them up*, so we came up with some examples of how to accessorize them to make them hot, but keep you from ruining your morning by overloading your breakfast and giving yourself a giant case of OWL Syndrome*.

Egg Example #1 - Have It Hard

Yep. Just keep it simple and try a good old-fashioned hard boiled egg - like the kind the Easter bunny hides (but throw yours out if they start to get any weird colors on them like his do). If you don't know how to hard boil an egg, we feel sorry for you, but since we're really nice, we'll talk you through it.

Fill a small pot with water. Put 4 to 6 eggs in the pot and make sure the water covers them. (*Note: Be sure to place the eggs gently into the pot; don't drop them like it's hot. The idea is not to have scrambled eggs sitting in a bucket of water.)* Then turn on the heat until the water boils, turn down the heat and let them boil for about 10-15 minutes. Put the eggs immediately into the fridge to let them cool, and the next morning you will have perfect little individually wrapped breakfasts! How hot is that? These are good if you're running late to work but need something in your stomach before your long-ass morning commute. Just peel, shake on some salt and pepper, and enjoy!

Egg Example #2 - Steam It Up

Steaming an egg is also called "poaching" an egg if you want to sound fancy. And if you don't know what poaching is, we once again feel sorry for you that you did not have a mother or grandmother or a hot older sister that ever poached you an egg. Poached eggs are pretty cool. This is another very healthy way to cook eggs because you don't use any butter or oil or lard at all! You just boil water under the egg until it cooks to your liking. You know what? We're not gonna talk you through this one. Just go buy an egg poacher, read the directions, and have 1 or 2 with some healthy multigrain toast.

Egg Example #3 - Make It Messy

Sometimes the messier the sex, the better, right? That's why we stay away from those awful BMS* guys. Well the same is true with our little friend the egg. Just *scramble* it, girl! Scrambled eggs, if done properly, can be the bomb. Crack your eggs, pour in a little water or a little milk, add herbs and spices and veggies and maybe a tiny bit of cheese or some salsa and cook them in a pan sprayed with Pam. So hot, so good, and so healthy.

WARNING: Ordering scrambled eggs at a restaurant can sometimes be *too* messy - like that one-night-stand who forgot to tell you that he had an STD. (Don't you wish that guys came with nutrition facts?) Eggs from fucked up* places can also have hidden harmful ingredients. Don't be afraid to ask questions before you order - do you really want eggs scrambled with cream and milk and lard and oil and butter and MAYONAISE? We didn't think so.

Egg Example #4 - Flip, Fold And Squeeze

One of our favorite egg creations on the planet is the *omelet.* You can fit so much good stuff inside, and it's all held together in a delicious package. It's like that really hot guy that surprises you by being a total sweetheart and gets you all twitterpated*. Anyway, there are about as many kinds of omelets as there are types of guys - plain, veggie, meaty, Denver, Greek, Spanish, etc. And just like with guys, we think it's very important to sample them all so that you can figure out exactly what you like. But be careful - some omelets (and of course some guys) are just plain bad for you and should be avoided at all costs. Trust your hot little intuition on this one.

We feel that this is a time to absolutely add cheese to your eggs. Eating an omelet without cheese is like having a best friend who doesn't have a telephone. We just don't see how that can be fulfilling. But be smart! If you're having an omelet smothered in Swiss cheese, make sure to add some spinach and mushrooms. Or try tomato and onion with feta cheese. Or if cheddar is your thing, then add some broccoli.

Whatever you do, just leave out the meat girls! There is no need for ham, sausage, or bacon to be folded into your cheese covered eggs. Hot Chicks are not Atkins Chicks! Plus, brunch is supposed to combine two meals, not seven, so you can't eat everything.

Egg Example #5 - Hold Out!

As tempting as it may be for you, you must say "no" to *fried* eggs. They are bad for you and totally not worth it. (Kind of like dating a guy in a band. That always ends badly.) Why, oh, why would you fry your eggs when we just gave you four other ways to enjoy them that are way more fun?! Eggs can be cooked over easy and over medium and all over the place without being fried in oil! Again, ask questions, and if you're getting a seedy vibe from the place, skip the eggs entirely and order something else. You'll have more fun making eggs the next morning for you and your honey when you know exactly what's going into the damned pan.

Note: There are some days when you're either hung-over or in bed until 1 p.m. burning lots and lots of calories and by the time you finally eat something, nothing but eggs and cheese on a bagel will suffice. There's just something about the way the guy at a shitty deli can put those things together that makes them ridiculously delicious. In these instances, go for it. Remember that the egg was probably fried in a bunch of butter and that the bagel was probably buttered too. (Come to think of it, that's probably why they're so damned delicious. It's not the deli guy at all.) But when you're having breakfast in the mid-afternoon, you can splurge. Just have a giant pound of spinach for dinner to help you get rid of some of those toxins.

Bagels

We all know the sad news by now that bagels are not good for us. They have a lot of calories and not much nutritional value at all. What makes matters worse is the fact that all of the stuff that we like to put on our bagels is even more fucked up* than the bagels themselves! Cream cheese is just fatty nonsense and butter is even fattier nonsense. Jelly may have less fat, but it's just sugar, ladies. Plus, do you know how many calories jellies and jams have? About 50 calories per tablespoon! That's not so great!

And bagels are one of those evil foods that are basically a double negative - they're highly caloric *and* not very satisfying. Bummer. If you start your day with a giant bagel and cream cheese, an hour later you might find yourself seriously considering murdering the guy in the next cubicle so you can steal his donut. In this case, your bagel has stabbed you in the back like that bitch who made out with your boyfriend right in front of you - it has made you fat *and* left you hungry.

The only really brilliant advice we can offer here is that if you need a bagel, go ahead and get one with a thin schmear, eat half, and love it. (You don't have to get low fat cream cheese or anything, but you know how much of that crap they put on there at the deli? Scrape off half of it.) When you find yourself famished again hours before lunchtime, it's time to eat the other half (of the bagel, not the leftover cream cheese. That would be gross).

And please don't waste your time with whole wheat bagels or low carb bagels! (Unless you actually like them, but that would be kinda weird.) Yes, we know that they may have a little bit more fiber than regular bagels, but trust us - there are plenty of better ways to make your stomach freak out (in a good way) than by eating a gross bagel. Plus, those fibery bagels have just as many calories as the regular, yummy ones, so you're no kind of martyr for eating them. When you decide to treat yourself to a bagel, treat yourself to the real thing - just do it the Hot Chick's way.

Cereal

We will forever love Jerry Seinfeld for making it socially acceptable to eat cereal all day long, and to even order it at a restaurant for dinner. We LOVE cereal...perhaps a bit too much. In fact, this is one of those foods around which it is very hard for us to retain self-control. Whenever we buy a box, the entire thing disappears VERY quickly. We tried to solve this problem by buying only the super-healthy, fibery kind. We thought it would be less tempting, but that didn't work at all. We ate that whole box, too, and it's really hard to feel hot after eating a giant box of fiber.

One obvious trick is to never eat cereal directly out of the box. Go ahead and use a bowl, and splash some milk on there. (Skim or soy milk please; we promise you won't even notice the difference.) We highly recommend that you strive to get the milk to cereal ratio right the first time, because it's very easy for us to keep going back to the cupboard, thinking, "I have a little extra milk at the bottom of my bowl; let me just toss in a little more cereal," and then two minutes later, "Oops, now I'm left with some dry cereal here, let me just pour on a bit more milk..." This back and forth often doesn't end until the entire box is once again empty. So ladies - one bowlful and end it!

Also, we hope it's really obvious which cereals are not hot to eat even one bowl of, and those are the ones that list sugar as their #1 ingredient. Seriously, if you're gonna eat a cereal that looks like and tastes like and has the exact same ingredients as cookies, why not just eat cookies for breakfast? At least they'll taste better, and you'll save the calories from the milk.

Another easy way to tell which cereals you should stay away from is to just avoid all of the ones with a mascot. Toucan Sam, the Cocoa Puffs Bird, that mean old Trix Rabbit, the hallucinating Lucky Charms dude - they're all freaking crazy, and you don't want to end up strung out and addicted to cereal like them.

Salad For Breakfast?

No, we're not that nightmare hippie girl that Beck sings about, but you Hot Chicks CAN try to start your day in a majorly healthy way, and go ahead and eat a salad for breakfast. This can be used as a form of insurance if you know that you won't be able to get your greens in at any other time that day. A small warning, though - this sometimes leaves you totally perplexed about what to eat for lunch and dinner that day.

For example, you eat a giant salad for breakfast, and at noon you think, "I don't want ANOTHER salad, but I am pretty hungry right now, and since I started my day on such a good note, I don't want to mess it all up with a giant bowl of pasta." This might be a good time to splurge on a well-deserved piece of pizza, some healthy fish, or maybe a yummy sandwich. (See the next chapter for more on this!)

But if you really fucked up* the night before and ate a sleeve of Chips Ahoy or something, now's a really good time to make a good old breakfast salad. We're not saying you have to atone for your mistakes, but we promise that those breakfast greens will make you feel healthy and hotter in no time.

Brunch Bummers

We don't really think that Sex & the City revolutionized the world like some people do, but we *have* noticed a lot more tables of 4-5 women eating brunch together every Sunday. We like this tradition, even though most brunch foods are pretty fucked up*. It's okay, because brunch is technically two meals - *breakfast and lunch* - so it's acceptable to eat twice as many calories.

It is *not*, however, acceptable to eat 5 or 6 times as many calories that you would normally eat at breakfast or lunch. Many brunch foods are sneaky bastards, too, so make sure you check out our list of brunch foods that you should never eat before you meet up with your gal pals.

Brunch Bummer #1 - Hash Browns

Hash browns taste OKAY, but they certainly aren't worth the gigantic amount of fat and calories that most of them have. They may look and taste just like boring plain potatoes, but they are actually boring, plain potatoes that were cooked in oil, frozen, thawed out, and then reheated in oil once again. Of course we're gonna say that you should replace it with some salad or fruit, but honestly you'd be better off ordering some toast instead, or even some french fries that will at least be worth it.

Brunch Bummer #2 - Scones

We notice a lot of ladies ordering scones instead of biscuits or toast in the morning. They probably think it's ladylike and dainty and therefore healthier. Well, that's stupid. Most scones actually have about 500 calories, which is more than a McDonald's biscuit with bacon, egg and cheese! We think that those bland, rock hard scones make better weapons than pastries, so save some to throw at your ex-boyfriend's windshield, but don't even bother eating them.

Brunch Bummer #3 - Granola

Okay, this is a dumb move that a lot of girls make - they order a bowl of granola, yogurt and fruit for brunch, thinking that it will be better for them than pancakes and waffles and other stuff that actually tastes good. The fruit and yogurt is cool, but granola is so, so fucked up*! One bowl of it has about the same amount of calories as two giant waffles with butter and syrup glistening all over them. And honestly, which would you rather eat?

Brunch Bummer #4 - Oatmeal

Okay, you're right - oatmeal really is totally healthy and we already said that it's a great breakfast. You've got us there. But we don't think that brunch is really the time to be eating oatmeal. First of all, why spend about eight dollars in a restaurant when you can make it at home for more like fifty cents? Plus, when your friends are scarfing down french toast and cheesy omelets and you're staring down a bowl of gruel, you will definitely regret your choice. Order something fun and filling, and if you get hungry again before dinner, eat a giant pound of spinach.

Special Occasion Breakfasts

The other thing you can do at breakfast is just embrace the fact that you're gonna go crazy, and eat a giant, fattening meal. Now pay attention—this is definitely only allowed on weekends, and preferably when you wake up either with a nice young man in your bed or a terrible hangover (or both).

On these occasions, go to your favorite greasy spoon (bring him with you) and choose your poison. We like crazy, giant pancakes with M&M's baked right in the batter and a fuckload of whipped cream and sprinkles on top. You might opt instead for waffles with ice cream, or that cheesy-nonsense-filled omelet we spoke of earlier. Any of these items make a perfect special occasion breakfast.

If that bastard escapes before dawn, or you wake up hung-over alone (sorry, but it happens to the best of us) make sure that you still enjoy your breakfast! Don't let some loser stop you from getting some good eats. You might want to go to Dunkin' Donuts and get one of their yummy chocolate-chip muffins, or even better, eat some (or all) of that leftover chocolate cake from last night's party. Go ahead and enjoy every single bite, and then plan on eating a giant pound of spinach for dinner.

Coffee

We love coffee and are addicted to it, and we know that most of you are, too. Coffee is our friend and we see no reason to shy away from it. However, these days coffee has been bastardized beyond recognition, and it's becoming a problem. Stay away from those name brand blended sugary concoctions at all costs. The new "lite" versions are slightly better, but still be wary of the whipped cream and flavored options.

One ounce of the syrup that adds flavor to your coffee also adds about 80 extra calories! That's totally not worth it. Also do your best to avoid lattes, or anything involving the word "mocha." Those drinks aren't coffees, they're desserts, and have just as many calories as the worst of them.

A lot of girls fuck up* and order Chai Tea Lattes, too, but listen - just because something sounds Asian, that doesn't mean it's healthy. Chai Tea Lattes are actually just as bad for you as mochas, frapps, or even hot chocolate, but they don't have nearly as much caffeine as coffee, so what's the point?

And don't for a minute think about ordering one of those disgusting green tea smoothies that they're selling these days at the coffee places. Yes, green tea is healthy, but anything blended with a carton of cream and a cup of sugar loses every bit of its nutritional value, so forget it.

Trust us; you can totally enjoy your coffee in its simplest form. Get the good stuff, not gas-station sludge. If you can take it black, then you might be even hotter than us. Kudos. But if you're not that advanced, no worries; neither are we. We know that a lot of you are pouring buckets of skim milk into your coffee in fear that half and half will make you fat. Stop it. Half and half is cool. It tastes way better than skim milk, doesn't make your coffee grey, and you'll look like a carefree, hot little vixen when you reach for it every morning.

Remember, coffee helps us out in a few ways - it makes our stomachs freak out (in a good way) and it even speeds up our metabolisms a little. The way we figure it, we *have* to use half and half just to balance out these other effects. Otherwise, we might just disappear.

Now for the question of sweeteners - this is a tough one. We definitely advise against regular sugar, because a few tablespoons of it is gonna start to make your coffee kind of fucked up*. But we totally understand if you guys are scared of the alternative packets of rat poison. It is a bit of a conundrum and we Hot Chicks really don't like making decisions, so our new favorite thing in America is Splenda!

Splenda doesn't taste like chemicals, sweetens your coffee up beautifully, and best of all, Splenda hasn't been proven to cause cancer yet! How awesome is that? We're sure that they're injecting it into hamsters somewhere right now and we're gonna get some bad news about the effects soon, so we're planning on using as much of it as we can now before it's too late!

Now, if you're totally obsessed with those delicious frappucinos and absolutely must have one, we totally understand. We just got out of rehab for this addiction ourselves. Once in a while (like, maybe once a week) it's okay to go for it. Get a big one, top it off with lots of whipped cream, and then (this is one of our absolute favorite Hot Chicks tricks) pour on some of that vanilla and chocolate powder that they so kindly leave sitting out by the milk and stuff.

Now, be very careful not to breathe in the powder as you sip because you'll probably choke on it, and it's hard to look hot when you're choking, even for the hottest of us. But remember, on the days you choose to do this at breakfast, you know what you're having for lunch—a giant pound of spinach.

10 Things That Smell Better Than They Taste

You know what we mean - this stuff smells so delicious that you just have to eat it, but once you do you instantly wonder why you ever wanted it in the first place! Here are a few sneaky ones to avoid:

#1 - Hot Dogs

They smell salty and hardly like meat at all, which we love, but who wants to really ingest processed mysterious meat chunks that don't resemble any animal we've ever seen? Certainly not a Hot Chick.

#2 - Popcorn

It smells SO good when the girl in the next cubicle pops it every afternoon that you're tempted to get your own bag, but once you start eating it it's never the same. Plus, let all of your other coworkers hate that other girl when they get sick of the smell in a few weeks.

#3 - Fried Chicken

Actually, most fried foods smell really good, but they're just simply not worth it. Plus, that smell can stick to your clothes and stay in your hair for days after you eat this stuff, which definitely isn't hot.

#4 - Cotton Candy

It's fun to get cotton candy when you're at a fair, but the smell is certainly better than the reality of eating it. If it's even the slightest bit windy you'll soon have fluffy sugar in your hair, on your clothes and stuck all over your face. Why not buy that weird cotton candy flavored perfume instead and keep yourself together?

#5 - Mall Pretzels

They smell awesome, but those glistening buttery twists that are sitting under fluorescent lighting never taste so great once you've spent $4 on one that could have been better spent on a cute pair of earrings.

#6 - Cinnabon

These are so tempting, with their cinnamon aroma and yummy-looking frosting, and yes, they actually do taste pretty damn good, too. But no taste in the whole world can make up for the amount of calories in these bad boys. One Cinnabon has 730 calories. That is just crazy. If you eat one of these today at the mall, you may have to go back tomorrow to buy a whole new wardrobe in a bigger size, which probably isn't worth it.

#7 - Funnel Cake

Again with the fried food. Funnel cake smells amazing, but once you've eaten this giant block of fried bread, you'll pretty much want to throw up instantly. We'll pass, thanks.

#8 - Coffee

Yes, we love coffee and already said that you should totally drink it, but you Hot Chicks should probably drink 1 or 2 cups of coffee a day, not 7. All we're trying to say here is that you shouldn't feel obliged to order another cup every time you get a whiff of that delicious fresh-brewed aroma.

#9 - Fresh Baked Bread

Bread is fine - we're not Atkins bitches! But you don't need to eat a whole loaf just because it smells so good while it's baking. Self control, ladies.

#10 - Street Nuts

These are also available at fairs, and they smell so good honey-roasting on a cold day. But once they're in a little plastic packet in your hand, all of the glamour is somehow gone and you'd probably be better off with a jar of Planters that is at least definitely uncontaminated by the street guy who sold them to you.

Chapter 2
How to Eat Like a Hot Chick
At Lunch

Lunch is tricky. We're usually starving by this point, and if you're hot like us, then you're probably also busy and don't have a lot of time to plan ahead. Also, we hate to say it, but it's not particularly hot to pack a lunch the night before in a brown paper sack, or even a cool little retro lunchbox. Sorry, girls, but you knew that, right? Face it, basically any food in the entire world is going to seem more appealing come lunchtime than the lukewarm saran-wrapped meal that's been sitting in your desk drawer for four hours. Luckily, it's not too hard to find lunches that are just as healthy and economical, and far more attractive. Here are our tips for making your lunch hour the hottest one of the day.

Salad

Lunch is the perfect time for salad, and it is very often that we end up at the salad bar mid-day. If you think that salad is boring, think again, bitches, because you obviously haven't explored salad's full potential. Salad bars these days are unbelievable. If you're lucky enough to live near a Whole Foods or another awesome grocery store like that, you have an amazing number of lunch options right there at their salad bar. But please be careful! It is very tempting to combine all of those numerous lunches into ONE GIANT, FUCKED UP* SALAD. We have made this mistake countless times, and so we have created several salad bar rules that every Hot Chick out there must follow.

Salad Rule #1 – No Scoop Of Hummus

Hummus always looks so nice and creamy in the tub that we're tempted to scoop a little of it onto our greens. This always backfires, so don't do it, ladies! Hummus is great on its own or with baby carrots dipped into it or something, but in the midst of a salad, its flavor and consistency are compromised, and it becomes a giant, gloppy mess. It is now a complete waste of calories, not to mention weight. Salad bars charge by the pound, girls, and the thick, sludgy stuff is heavy. Save it for another time.

Salad Rule #2 - No Hot Food

We break this rule all the time. It's just that the hot food items on the salad bar look so much more appealing than the cold salad stuff. You've got lettuce and tuna and sliced mushrooms on your plate, and then you see the eggplant parmesan and the vegetable curry, and you think, "A small piece of eggplant might go nicely on my salad...and maybe I'll top it all off with some cauliflower from the curry to give it a little extra zing." This always ends badly. When faced with this scenario, eat your salad as it is, and then go have eggplant parmesan or vegetable curry for dinner. But not both!! You would never eat both in one meal, so don't start now.

Salad Rule #3 - No Crunchy Toppings

You know what we're talking about here—those yummy sesame sticks that have like 50 calories each, and sunflower seeds that are supposedly good for you but have more fat than Haagen-Dazs. We have no problem with these foods on their own, and if you want to snack on them after lunch, go ahead. But why put them on the salad? You'll barely notice them, and these calories are better spent elsewhere.

Salad Rule #4 - No Olive Oil

We hope you already know to avoid typical bottled dressings that have a ridiculous number of fat and calories. So then why are so many of you still drenching your salads in olive oil? We detest olive oil, despite Rachael Ray's cute little acronym

(EVOO) and its bullshit reputation for curing cancer. Would you rather have olive oil on your salad, or save those calories and have a piece of chocolate cake later? Exactly. If you can find a light bottled dressing you can stand that doesn't have a lot of calories, go for it. Otherwise, do what we do and just use a ton of balsamic vinegar, which has practically no calories and adds some really intense flavor. But for God's sake, ladies, if you're gonna ruin your salad with olive oil, do us all a favor and go eat a cheeseburger instead.

It IS Easy Eating Greens!

Okay, we know what you're thinking – "So what the hell AM I allowed to put on my salad?" Don't worry; we have plenty of ways to make them tasty without breaking any of our rules. First of all, choose your greens smartly. Hot Chicks do not eat iceberg lettuce. That's right – no more giant green bowling balls for you girls.

Instead, go for those pretty baby greens, spinach, arugula, or any combination of this stuff. Romaine is okay too, but we think the hardcore greens are hotter. They pack far more vitamins and fiber and all that good stuff, have practically no calories, and really do have a lot more flavor than iceberg or romaine. And don't worry about the latest headlines about E. Coli-tainted spinach or any of that nonsense. Spinach is good for you, and a little E. Coli never hurt anyone. It'll probably just make your stomach freak out for a few days, and then you won't have to worry about doing that gross maple syrup cleanse that your best friend swears by any time soon.

Another important trick is to season your greens. Always use a little salt. Salt is awesome. Find other ways to lower your blood pressure, like yoga. Also, be adventurous and use seasonings that you wouldn't ordinarily think of putting on a salad, like basil or rosemary, or even those bottled seasoning blends. They will definitely make your salad taste better. (And yes, you can go ahead and yell "bam!" as you throw your spices in, if that does something for you.)

Composing The Best Salad

Okay, the essential components to any good salad include any and all raw vegetables you can possibly think of, plus some healthy form of protein, like tofu, tuna (not tuna SALAD, ladies, just the plain tuna), beans, or even chicken. We've recently discovered that chicken makes us itchy. Maybe we're allergic? Any kind of itchiness is obviously far from hot, so we're currently avoiding it, but you go ahead and eat it.

Once you've got your basics down, you can take advantage of the salad bar, and go ahead and throw in a little bit of some of the other items that look good. If there's some pasta salad that you can't resist but know is probably fucked up*, just put a little tiny bit on your salad. If there's a tub of grilled or roasted vegetables, take a few of those. This customization is the beauty part of a salad bar, so make sure to take advantage.

Get creative. Guacamole is good on salad, and in moderation is actually pretty healthy. Salsa is also a great topping, adds tons of flavor, and has very few calories. You can even have fun with it and make a "theme salad." We recently surprised ourselves by creating a veritable Mexican fiesta at the salad bar—lettuce, black olives, salsa, guacamole, goat cheese and black beans. Ole! See? Salad really can be hot.

Cheese

We love having cheese in our lives and on our salads, but we also know that most kinds of cheeses are really fucked up*. Hot Chicks put only two kinds of cheese on their salads—goat cheese (or feta, but that's really the same thing) and parmesan. Our reasoning is simple: these two cheeses have the fewest calories, the least amount of fat, and are both really, really tasty. Parmesan cheese is one of our favorite things on the planet, and we put it on almost everything. Even the ugly, giant green canister they put it in doesn't diminish its hotness.

What's Up With This Pound Of Spinach?

Some of you may be confused as to why we keep telling you to eat a pound of spinach. We know that it possibly sounds a bit ridiculous and disgusting, but we also know that it is a kick-ass food that will help you feel and look your hottest. Popeye was one smart mother f'er. And just like Popeye, spinach is hot even without Olive Oil!

Spinach has only 30 calories per cup and a giant fuckton of nutrition. It is a very rich source of iron, calcium potassium, folate, vitamins K, A, C, B1, B2, B3, B6, and even has some of those omega 3 fatty acids that are so great for our metabolisms. It's also got amazing antioxidants that will help keep us hot and wrinkle-free for years, and may help protect our hot little asses from osteoporosis, heart disease, colon cancer and arthritis.

This super-food is also full of fiber. Fiber is what keeps us regular. And being regular (as gross as it is to talk about poo) is what makes us feel like our tummies are flat and fabulous. Spinach is also an anti-inflammatory, so it's awesome for those times of the month when we're carrying around pounds of extra water weight, or after a night of drinking when even our ankles are swollen from too many beers.

Spinach is truly the cornerstone of the Hot Chicks Diet. The stuff is just unbelievable, and it tastes pretty damn good too. If you did not like spinach as a kid, then your mamma probably made it wrong. Sorry, but you have to trust us on this. Taste buds change every seven years, so give it another shot. Just don't buy a giant clump of leafy raw spinach that is full of dirt and mud. We like to know that our food came from the earth, but we don't want to eat the earth along with it. Also, please don't buy canned spinach. That shit is kinda gross and has just as much sodium as a bag of Cheetos.

Instead, buy some pretty baby spinach in bags and use it for salads. (See our Salad Bar Rules for more info!) It will fill you up and instantly make you feel like you're eating like a Hot Chick. Or buy blocks and blocks of frozen spinach and microwave it with salt, I can't believe it's not butter and parmesan cheese for an awesome nutrient boost along with any meal! You will immediately start glowing, and if you ate something crappy 5 hours earlier, all the fiber from the spinach will grab all those nasty toxins and push them through you quicker. How hot is that?

Sandwiches

We don't get it, but it seems that most people eat these weird things for lunch every day. We just don't like them. Well, okay, we admit that there are a couple of good ones - fluffernutters, peanut butter and jelly...anything with peanut butter, really. Then again, peanut butter is good on anything, anytime, anyplace. And now that we're on the subject, wouldn't a giant jar of the stuff with a spoon be way more fun than schmeering it on bread?

Anyway, a lot of sandwiches that taste good are actually fucked up*. Either they were grilled in lots of butter and oil, or whoever made it snuck a bunch of mayo in there just to mess with you. This is why it's always safer to make these things yourself. Of course, there are some sandwiches that aren't totally bad for you, but these are often the boring ones. You know what we're talking about—sprouts on whole wheat or cucumber on toast. Don't waste your time here. Plus, it's hard to look hot when you're stuffing a 12-inch hoagie into your mouth. Put down those sandwiches, ladies, and pick up your knife and fork. It's totally worth the effort.

Okay, we may sound a little too passionate about the sandwich thing, but Hot Chicks are passionate about everything. And just because we try to stay away from them, that doesn't mean we don't have some good tips on how to work it out and create the best tasting and smartest sandwiches on the planet. So if you do decide to eat one, these are our magic* tricks for not making your lunch stick to your hips.

Sandwich Trick #1 - ONLY "WHOLE GRAIN" BREAD!!

This is serious, ladies. If you have white Wonder Bread in your house, we want to know why. Actually, never mind; just throw it away right this instant! There are so many preservatives and strange, scary ingredients in that crap that you might as well just wrap bologna around a twinkie and call it lunch. And just so you know, regular wheat breads are also made with white flour, so that's no good either.

Look for breads that say "Whole Grain" and only have ingredients that you can pronounce. The switch might take a minute or two to get used to, but very soon you'll be loving it! Choose bread with lots of nuts and seeds and oats, and different kinds of grains like rye and spelt and amaranth (guess you'll need to learn how to pronounce that). This will give your sandwich fiber, vitamins, minerals and a texture as good as sprinkles on frozen yogurt or stubble on a hot guy's face.

Sandwich Trick #2 - NO MAYO, or That Fake Miracle Whip Stuff!

DON'T DO IT! It's not worth it! We definitely don't think that buying jars of fatty, oily egg yolks is hot. It's ridiculously high in calories, has zero nutritional value, and if you use all of our sandwich tricks, we promise that you won't miss it. The Hot Chick trick to keeping your sandwich moist and full of flavor (while avoiding mayo) is to add a *ton of mustard.* We love mustard! The regular kind, the fancy deli-style crap, whatever - they all have no more than 10 calories per two whole tablespoons, and are bursting with flavor.

Don't like mustard? You're insane, but fine, try spreading hummus on that healthy bread of yours. (*CAUTION: Read your ingredients. Don't get the hummus made with oil, or you're back to the caloric level of mayo.*) A thin layer of hummus on your bread will make your sandwich so moist and so yummy that you won't know what to do with yourself. Really. You'll have no idea.

We know there are a great number of you out there who go to those super fun delis for lunch and get some sort of crazy cream cheese concoction on your sandwich. Even though it's just as fattening as mayo, we will support the cream cheese thing *occasionally,* just because we know how much fun it is. However, if you want to feel hot and you're having cream cheese on your sandwich at lunch, then you should be eating apples and spinach for breakfast and dinner.

NOTE: We know some of you are freaking out right now, thinking, "Wait! What about tuna salad or chicken salad sandwiches?" Do us a favor and try mixing your tuna or chopped chicken (if it doesn't make you itchy like us) with mustard or a spoonful of non-fat plain yogurt or even some of that yummy hummus. It's actually really good! Then add a ton of fun spices like dill and garlic and crazy peppers. In the words of that nutty bitch Rachael Ray, "Yum-O!"

Sandwich Trick #3 - Choose Your Meat As Carefully As You'd Choose A Boyfriend (Or Girlfriend...We Don't Discriminate)

Hot Chicks don't fake it. That goes for everything, but especially your deli meats. Go for the real thing - none of this fake, processed nonsense that's coated with poisons and disguised as meat. All of that packaged crap has been treated with hormones and preservatives, and is loaded with nitrates and enough sodium to make you swell up like "Violet" in *Willie Wonka and the Chocolate Factory*.

Go to your neighborhood deli or to your favorite supermarket, and get your meat sliced fresh. If you are lucky enough to live near a health food store, they have meat that's completely free of all the bad stuff. Also, do we really need to even remind you to choose *lean* meats like turkey over pastrami and salami? You can have a giant Philly Cheese Steak *occasionally* (hopefully when you're actually in Philadelphia), but if you're eating sandwiches for lunch every day, then we recommend that you start making hotter choices.

NOTE: Try grilled tofu or half an avocado instead of meat. Seriously, it's good. No, really. We promise. Seriously.

Sandwich Trick #4 - Accessorize!!

This is the fun part, and the trick to making your sandwich satisfy you for hours after you've eaten it. Have you ever gone to get a giant tuna melt on you lunch break, eaten the whole damn thing, and then been pissed off afterwards because you were still hungry? Start eating sandwiches like a Hot Chick and that will never happen again.

The trick is to follow some of the same salad rules. Add a ton of lettuce, spinach, sliced cucumbers, tomatoes, roasted peppers, sprouts if you can handle them, onions if you don't have a date later, a few olives, a few pickles, and maybe even some mushrooms. This will make it filling and nutritious, without adding any calories. Now *that's* hot. Pour on some balsamic vinegar (no oil!) and spices like basil and oregano over those veggies, and we promise your sandwich will taste as good as the pheromones of that guy you have crazy chemistry with.

NOTE: This is not the best "date food," because properly accessorizing will leave you with a sandwich that is giant, shaky, leaking and overflowing with goodness. Mustard might squirt in your eye, vinegar will drip down your chin, and pickles might land on your lap. You'll probably find all sorts of goodies later when you take your bra off, too.

Wait, you want to add cheese to the list of accessories? *Hmmmm.* Well, no, uh-uh, you can't. Seriously, think about it. After you do all the other tricks, will you even be able to taste the cheese? Not really, and it's gonna add like 200 calories. But if you still have to have it, choose wisely. Feta and Parmesan are great options, and some low fat Swiss isn't that bad either, but PLEASE, don't even think about adding those individually wrapped slices of yellow processed plastic. That stuff is not cheese. It's just insane.

Sandwich Trick #5 - Don't Be Fooled!

All those yellow, blue and green sub-sandwich chains are just disgusting fast food joints with things like "Fresh," "Healthy" and "Just Baked" painted on their windows. We could paint all sorts of nice things about ourselves on our front doors, but that wouldn't necessarily make them true. The subs at these places may have fewer calories than a Jumbo Jack, but so does a Snickers bar.

And as for that fat loser Jared losing ten sizes eating just two Subs a day... *come on!!!* Think about it! If you just ate 2 of *anything* a day you'd loose weight. Eat two Hagaan Dazs bars, at 500 calories each, and that's only 1,000 calories for the day. You'd totally lose weight. Eat two slices of pizza a day and nothing else, or two boxes of Milk Duds, and yep, you'll probably lose weight, too, but you'll hate the world and you won't feel hot. We promise.

Anyway, all those sandwiches are filled with meats and cheeses that are completely processed with chemicals, hormones and additives that are as bad for you as a married man. And that "Fresh Baked" Bread? That is a joke, ladies, and not a funny one. That dough is just batter in a barrel that is shipped in on a giant truck and poured into a pan and put in an oven by a 16 year old who's making $6 an hour. We're not saying that you can *never* eat at these places, but please be aware of the facts. Again, smart chicks are Hot Chicks!

Soup It Up

Haven't you heard about all those recent studies proving that soup can help us lose weight? It has something to do with the amount of liquid involved; it makes our bellies feel full. Anyway, soup is pretty cool, especially in the middle of winter when even frozen yogurt isn't appealing. Just kidding! What are we, crazy? Frozen yogurt is never unappealing, even on the coldest day of the year. Anyway, right, we were talking about soup. Soup can make a decent, warming lunch, but of course you have to be careful.

First of all, your soup has to have a lot of stuff in it in order to make it really satisfying. Make sure yours has beans or giant chunks of vegetables, or even noodles or rice or alphabet bits if you want. But if you go for a bean soup, don't joke around with that sour cream they plop on top. That's like dolloping an extra chin on top of your soup. Chili isn't a bad option, but please don't ever buy one of those little packaged chili tubs that you heat in the office microwave. We all know that the office microwave is coated with layers upon layers of your co-workers' lunches for the last 15 years, which is obviously anything but hot.

We assume that you all know that your soup base must be broth-y or vegetable-y, but here is a reminder of some soup terms to avoid all costs: bisque, chowder, roux, and most importantly – CREAM OF. This part ain't rocket science, girls. No cream soups.

You do, however, have our full permission to crumble as many crackers as you can fit into your soup bowl. We know that the whole texture contrast thing is crucial for providing a satisfying soup experience, and crackers also have the ability to transform soup into a full meal.

However, you *must* use these crackers in lieu of croutons. Croutons are actually fried. Fried! Can you believe that crap? We're eating soup here; we're trying to be healthy, and some smartass decided to throw tiny fried bread chunks in our bowl just to mess with us! But we Hot Chicks cannot be fooled, and this is precisely the kind of thing we're here to protect you from.

Bars

Sometimes when we're really short on time during lunch, we find ourselves tempted to replace the meal with those god-awful bars. But why, why, why would we really want to eat something that has been processed and condensed down into a bar shape, and resembles nothing that can be found in nature? Plus, these gritty, dust-flavored bars aren't exactly the health panaceas they are marketed to be - they're actually kind of fucked up*.

For the same number of calories there are in a typical bar, you can eat something like five apples, three bananas, or two avocados mashed up into some really yummy guacamole. Get our point? And seriously, if you're gonna eat anything with the word "bar" in the title, please just make it chocolate!

Pizza

Let's face it, everyone loves pizza. It's quick, it's cheap, and there are no dirty plates or utensils to wash afterwards. We're not exactly huge fans of doing dishes, so pizza scores several points with us right there. A lot of ladies don't eat pizza as a rule, because they assume that it's terrible for them, but we don't like to rule things out entirely. We know that if we do that, one day we'll end up getting dumped or fired and we'll find ourselves dazed and confused and doing some major damage at the all-you-can-eat Pizza Hut lunch buffet. That would be bad.

We're gonna go ahead and make one hard and fast pizza rule, though. NO CHAIN PIZZA. Yep, you heard us—no Pizza Hut, no Dominos, definitely no Pizzeria Uno. If you live in a town where this is the only type of pizza available, then we're very sorry, but you won't be eating any pizza. It's simple: this stuff isn't really pizza; it's fast food, and Hot Chicks don't consciously eat fast food (more on this later).

But if you've found a nice independently owned and operated pizza joint in your 'hood, you can eat lunch there every once in a while. Not every day. But on those days when you've had a healthy breakfast and you choose pizza for lunch, then you're damned well going to enjoy it.

Don't worry - we're not going to tell you to blot all of the extra oil off the top like some diet books would. You'll just end up sitting next to a giant pile of soggy napkins, and your pizza will look like it just shaved, with little tissue bits all over its face. Not hot, ladies, not hot. Instead, here's how we Hot Chicks do it:

We order giant slices (not a whole PIE) with lots of veggie toppings. Sorry, but no pepperoni or sausage allowed. Seriously, it's pizza; you don't need animal lard making it worse. So load on your fave veggies, and then sprinkle on a little bit of garlic powder, a few crushed red pepper flakes, and (this is the best part) a TON of Parmesan cheese! Just go ahead and shake it on every single bite, including the crust. Trust us; this move is so hot that the universe* will simply not allow it to make us fat.

And Now A Word On Fast Food:

We aren't going to spend a lot of time on this. There is just nothing hot whatsoever about any single fast food establishment, or any of the ridiculously fucked up food that they serve. Food shouldn't be defined by its speed. Go see SUPERSIZE ME, and read FAST FOOD NATION if you need specifics here, but you have to admit that you already know the truth about this garbage by now.*

Suffice it for us to say that if you absolutely must east fast food of any kind, at least do it at three a.m., when you're completely wasted and won't remember it in the morning. We're pretty sure that things we don't remember eating can't actually affect our bodies in any way.

If you're confused about what exactly constitutes fast food, use the same cereal test and avoid all restaurants that have mascots. We mean, do you really want to look like Ronald McDonald, Long John Silver, that freaky Bob's Big Boy kid, or (God forbid) the Grimace? And what the heck is the Grimace, anyway - a purple Klansman? We have no clue, but we do know that he's fat, weird, and definitely not hot.

*10 Things That Are Secretly Magic**

You know how magical spinach is, and we've told you why we think Splenda is cool, but try adding these awesome things into your life, and you'll be even hotter!

#1 - Cayenne Pepper

This stuff is so cool. You may not know this, but spicy foods are known to boost your metabolism! So, if you like it hot, try adding a dash of cayenne pepper to soups, salads, fish, and whatever else you want to have a little extra kick. Throw out that salty Tabasco sauce and use this instead. It has no calories, and in addition to speeding up your metabolism, it supposedly aids digestion, improves circulation, and is good for the sinuses and all the major organs.

#2 - Cinnamon

We're not talking about cinnamon coffee cake, gum or cinnamon gummy bears. We mean pure cinnamon, from the bark. Sprinkle it in your coffee or tea and stir it into oatmeal or yogurt. Cinnamon is good for all sorts of things like yeast infections and nausea (gross), but we love it because it help keeps us hot! Cinnamon enhances the metabolism of fats! Yay!

#3 - Apple Cider Vinegar

Okay, it may not be as yummy as balsamic, but this stuff is super good for our hot little bods. It has all of the nutrients that apples have, but like zero calories. So pour it on your salad with a few other spices, and notice your extra high energy level as your tummy flattens.

#4 - Flax

This is another magical addition to the Hot Chick diet. Flax promotes healthy skin, nails and teeth, and is great for inflammation and constipation (sorry, gross). So if your nails are breaking and you feel bloated all the time, add flax seeds to oatmeal or cereal, or make it a topping for frozen yogurt. Fun! You can drink flax oil if you want to, but we think the tiny crunchy seeds are a bit easier to swallow.

#5 - Alfalfa

Many people hate alfalfa sprouts, but we need to tell you how good they are for you and how easy it is to add them into your life. Just throw a bundle onto your salad or into your sandwich and make yourself eat them. Alfalfa helps detoxify the body, balance hormones, and it acts as a diuretic and helps with inflammation. This is all totally necessary for a Hot Chick - especially when we're PMS-ing!

#6 - Fish Oil

We know you're out there! You're a Hot Chick and you hate fish. The smell, the taste, the thought - all of it disgusts you. Well, you're in luck, because we can now get all of the slimming benefits of salmon and other fish in a cute little fish oil pill.

Fish oil has Omega-3 Fatty Acids (which are the good fats, so don't freak out). These "good fats" not only help keep our lovely hearts healthy, but they keep our skin glowing and our thighs shrinking. We don't care how you swallow it; just make sure you're getting your fish oil somehow!

#7 - Green Tea

If you've watched Oprah at all in the last two years, we're sure you've seen an episode where she raves about the benefits of Green Tea. Well she's right, as usual. Oprah and Green Tea are the bomb! Besides boosting metabolism and helping with fatigue, it may lower your risk of cancer! So if you smoke and drink and sunbathe and down diet coke by the case, you should have a cup of green tea a day. It can only make you hotter!

#8 - Fennel

You may be thinking, "What the fuck is fennel?" Well, there are fennel berries, roots, and stems, which means that you can buy fennel like any other spice and sprinkle it on your food. Or, you can get fennel tea and drink it, which is how we like to consume it! Get this, girls - fennel is a natural appetite suppressant and it decreases sugar cravings! It's also good for the kidneys and all of your other organs. But we like it for the former, because it helps us during those tough times. Drink a cup after lunch and dinner and it'll help with cravings and you'll totally feel hotter. It's weird, but it works.

#9 - Rosemary

This magic herb is also really yummy. Have you ever have rosemary bread or chicken grilled with rosemary? Well, we love it. We get really bored with food sometimes, and cooking with rosemary is a great way to change things up. It not only makes your food taste like it's from a five star restaurant, but it's good for all sorts of other things - rosemary fights bacteria, is great for circulation and digestion, and it helps with headaches and menstrual cramps. How hot is that?

10 - Chocolate

No, ladies. This does not mean you have an excuse to eat hot fudge every day. Most chocolate is full of sugar, which is what makes our magic jeans too tight. But chocolate in its pure form is actually really good for us. It has all sorts of antioxidants that prevent certain cancers and keep our arteries from clogging, and chemicals like phenyl ethylamine, which give us the same pleasure as a hot round of sex! So have a little square of dark chocolate, the kind with the highest cocoa content and least amount of sugar, and you will be one happy Hot Chick.*

Chapter 3
How to Snack Like a Hot Chick
All Day Long

Don't listen to those idiots who tell you not to eat between meals. That's so lame. Eating between meals is possibly the most fun part of the day. Plus, eating lots of snacks all day long is what prevents us from getting way too hungry and eating the first thing we see when we get home, whether it's a basket of bread or a giant tin of three-flavored popcorn. However, in order to be hot you definitely have to be smart about exactly what you snack on. Your snacks should not have more calories than your dinner, or you're totally fucking up*. Here are some good (and bad) ideas.

Frozen Yogurt

Frozen Yogurt is probably our favorite thing on the planet. Literally. When our friend asked us once if we'd rather have frozen yogurt every day or good sex, we were seriously torn. Come to think of it, we still don't know what we'd choose, and we aren't two of those lame girls who don't enjoy sex, either. Again, that's why we don't date guys with giant (or small) cases of BMS*.

Anyway, frozen yogurt is the best. It's freaking delicious and you can eat a lot of it for very few calories. The one easy way to mess it up, though, is with toppings. A few scoops of chopped nuts and carob chips or even sprinkles, and the calories start approaching pizza-like proportions.

For a while there we tried to solve this problem by ordering our toppings on the side. Self control escaped us, though, and sometimes we ended up eating the entire cup of topping with a spoon once we were out of frozen yogurt. Eating an entire cup of topping is kind of like sleeping with that cute boy who you know won't take you for pancakes the next morning or call you again until he's feeling heydayish*. It's good at the time, but it's totally unsatisfying and you always end up feeling like total crap afterwards. We definitely mess up and make both mistakes on occasion, but we try not to make either one a regular habit.

Our current solution is to ask for a LITTLE bit of topping on our yogurt, so that we get the fun consistency and don't feel deprived. Hot Chicks never deprive themselves of anything, and we would never REALLY deprive ourselves of frozen yogurt OR sex, but the thought of it is really horrifying. It's a terrible self destructive fantasy sequence* that we engage in once in a while, like our own personal version of *Sophie's Choice.*

Candy

We were once told by a good friend of ours that we have a "candy problem." Ex-CUSE us? We believe that SHE is actually the one with the problem, because she doesn't know how to appreciate a fun, sugary snack from time to time. Another one of our favorite things on the planet is bulk candy, because you can pick and choose from a variety of sweets without committing to buying (and then eating) an entire bag of each. Not eating an entire bag of chocolate kisses is essential to snacking like a Hot Chick.

Now, we've already established that we don't have a ton of self-control, so we can't take the word "bulk" in the bulk candy too literally. We scoop out just a few of each item (a couple of sour patch kids, a few M&M's, maybe one or two malted milk balls), enjoy them then and there and move on.

The best part is, most markets with bulk candy bins also have an unofficial free sample policy! You can always grab one or two yogurt covered pretzels while you fill your basket with healthy fruits and veggies. Hot Chicks would never advocate shoplifting, but we do think that whatever happens in the bulk food aisle stays in the bulk food aisle.

Chips

We don't often get a hankering for salty, crunchy chips, but we totally understand that some of you do. We can get behind that. Most chips have a ton of hydrogenated crap in them, though, so please be careful when buying your chips. Two pretty cool ones are Lay's plain potato chips and Fritos. Did you know that both of those are actually all natural and have only like 3 ingredients? We think that's pretty awesome, but still be conscious of how many you eat, because one of those ingredients is definitely a fuckload of oil.

Anyway, on days that you do choose to indulge, whatever you do, do not pour a small serving into a tiny bowl. Only LSE* girls do this. It's not fun, and it's definitely not hot. We know that part of the deal is digging around in the bag and picking out the chips that look the crispiest, or the biggest, or the smallest, or whatever *your* thing is, so do that. You'll only end up pouring another serving into the bowl, and then ANOTHER, so don't waste the dirty dish on such garbage.

Fruit

We HATE Atkins. Seriously, what an idiot. Sorry, but he's dead anyway, and really, a diet that makes you live in mortal fear of a banana just plain doesn't make sense. And trust us, eating pork rinds and fried meat all day is definitely not gonna make you feel (or look) hot. Fruit, on the other hand, *is* hot. It has the highest number of nutrients per calorie of any food on the planet (seriously, we looked it up) and it's really yummy.

All fruits are good and they're so healthy that you can totally squirt some whipped cream on there, or sprinkle on a little sugar, and it's no problem. Some particularly hot fruits are strawberries and papayas, which have tons of vitamins and help us digest all that spinach.

Another fruit tip is to freeze bananas, grapes, or any other fruit that sounds like fun. This is especially refreshing in the summer! Freezing fruit somehow concentrates the sugar, which makes it taste kinda like sorbet. Plus, as a co-worker of ours once said, (though it was actually kind of inappropriate) "A girl's always gotta have a frozen banana handy."

The only way for you to really fuck up* around fruit is to eat DRIED fruit, which is basically a bunch of condensed, wrinkly little calorie nuggets. We suppose dried fruit comes in pretty handy when you're hiking a giant mountain, or (let's be realistic) if your car breaks down on the way to Vegas, but it's a bad choice when there's juicy, fresh fruit around. Always make it a last resort.

Nuts

We're nuts about nuts. There. We said it.

Nuts are high in protein and good fats, so they are obviously healthy, but we all know that they are seriously fucked up*. It is crucial for Hot Chicks to be very, very careful around nuts in any form. It's quite easy to consume more calories than we realize just by picking around in some trail mix or hitting the cocktail-party assortment.

The trick is to be aware of what you're doing. Certain nuts are better than others. Peanuts, for example, are relatively low in calories (as long as they're not honey-roasted or anything). Almonds are another good choice, and are particularly high in protein. Pecans and walnuts are yummy, and not too bad for us in moderation, but again NO CANDIED NONSENSE. We have to be strict about that one.

The two nuts you must never, ever eat are the dreaded macadamia, and the brazil nut. One measly ounce of macadamias has 200 calories and 17 grams of fat! Even worse, each and every single brazil nut has over 25 calories! That's something like an extra five minutes on the exercise bike PER NUT. We like working out and everything, but we sure don't think that's worth it.

We Like Peanut Butter...

Okay, now, everyone has a few foods that they simply cannot have around the house. Diet experts call these "trigger foods." These are the items that you lose all self-control around, the ones that you will consume in their entirety if given the opportunity. We've already discussed our problem with cereal, but that doesn't even begin to rival the difficulty we have when we find ourselves in the proximity of a jar of peanut butter. Peanut butter is delicious. Creamy... salty...buttery. It's good stuff.

Now, we know we said that Hot Chicks don't deprive themselves, and that we don't rule out specific foods, yada, yada, yada, but this is one of our few exceptions. Every single time we have had peanut butter in our house, we have eaten the whole jar, which has about 3,000 calories. Seriously, we'd rather abstain from peanut butter entirely than gain a pound in a single sitting, so we don't buy the stuff at all any more. Ever.

If you can control yourself around peanut butter, be our guest and eat it in moderation on carrots or celery, or even have a spoonful right out of the jar. It makes a great snack. In fact, we're really jealous of you right now because you can do that. We recommend the all-natural kind, though, which doesn't have added sugar and fillers and additives like some of those "mom approved" brands.

Yogurt

Some of you may not understand our addiction to *frozen* yogurt, or you may not even have it available. (Damn. We feel bad for you.) But we know that all of you have heard that regular yogurt is a good diet food. Yogurt has been labeled a healthy snack for years, but we think that all those pretty little dairy maids are full of cow shit.

If you read the labels on those tiny plastic tubs, you would see that they actually have TONS of high fructose corn syrup, fake fruit, weird dyes, tons of sodium and a bunch of other crazy chemicals. We think that if you're gonna eat a bunch of crap like that, you should just indulge in a bag of sour patch kids or something.

Don't believe that a 6 ounce, 200 calorie carton of pink sugary cream is gonna make you hot. That's almost as many calories per ounce as ice-cream! And that tiny serving of yogurt also isn't going to make you feel full. As fast as you've scooped up all three spoonfuls, you'll end up just pulling a gallon of Breyers out of the old freezer and eating several more ounces of that. But trust us that you wouldn't be so tempted to do so if you had eaten a more filling snack like apples and nuts or two crackers with some cheese.

However, not *all* yogurts are bad. In fact, if you can get your pretty little non man-hands on the *real* stuff, then you're in for a treat. All those girls in Greece and Israel and Bulgaria eat gallons of the stuff every day, and those girls stay naturally hot for a long time. They even claim that yogurt is the secret to their flawless skin and flat tummies, and we actually kinda believe them.

Greek yogurt and other versions of organic plain yogurt are filled with tons of protein, good fat, and even have all those live cultures that help us with digestion. The bottom line is, yogurt can be a good snack, but remember that unlike most foods, yogurt is nothing like men. While we like our men as crazy and colorful as possible (just look at our boyfriend) with yogurt, the plainer the better!

Midnight Munchies

We think that all of those fairytale chicks must have had such flawless figures because they were safely tucked into bed when the clock struck twelve instead of snacking on a pint of Ben and Jerry's. Maybe that's what helped them fit into those tiny glass slippers and prevented them from turning into big giant pumpkins!

Well, we don't think those bitches had nearly as much shit to do in a day as we do. They did seem to have a lot of stress in their lives, but most of us don't have fairy godmothers or seven dwarfs to help us get through the day. Plus, Prince Charming always saved them from their debt and back taxes in the end anyway, and that hasn't happened to us yet.

Anyway, we realize that a lot of you Hot Chicks are either wide awake at midnight finishing up chores or partially awake on the couch watching endless Friends re-runs. Either way, if you ate dinner at 6 or 7 or even 8, by midnight, you're probably hungry again, and by the time Friends is over you'll be in the kitchen opening up all the cupboards and sticking your pretty heads in the fridge trying to come up with something fun to munch on.

Well, we did our research and found that when a chick starts eating in the middle of the night, she's likely to totally fuck up*. Many of us can eat well all day, and then as soon as the rest of the world is peacefully asleep, we loose all willpower and want to devour everything in sight. What's up with that?

It probably has something to do with our crazy female, hormonal emotions or loneliness or giant cases of OWL Syndrome.*

Whatever the deep rooted reason is, we know how hard it is to tame those maddening midnight munchies, but we also know how to keep you from "running for the border" at 1 a.m. Follow these 5 nighttime rules, and you too might wake up with a prince's tongue in your mouth instead of half of a soggy taco.

N - Never Eat Another Whole Meal

That's right, no matter how hungry you think you are at midnight, you really do not need to eat another giant meal. Unless you are pregnant, working the graveyard shift parking cars or burning 3,000 calories a day on Dancing with the Stars, you do not need two dinners. If your hunger pangs are keeping you awake and you still want to wake up with a flat tummy, you should eat *something*, but not everything. Don't reheat your pot roast and potatoes, finish off the rest of the pizza pie you started for dinner or even think about getting in your car and driving to Burger King! Those are not snacks, and you should know that by now.

I - Is It Bed Time?

Think girls - are you *really* hungry? Or are you just grumpy and tired and avoiding going to bed for some weird reason? Give that some long, hard thought before you pop that bag of buttery popcorn. It is very possible that if you just brush those pearly whites, put on your sexy nightie and get into your warm bed, you'll feel satisfied without eating anything.

G - Grab Something Small

Okay, so if you *are* really hungry and you *need* a midnight snack to survive, make it a *snack*. Snacks are *small* (100 to 200 calories). Have an apple dipped in some almond butter if you want a sweet taste, or have a piece of cheese, a couple of crackers and a pickle if you're craving something salty. Whatever you eat, make sure its snack sized, and you'll have much sweeter dreams than if you eat a dozen doughnuts.

H - Have A Drink

We're not really talking about alcohol here, but a little glass of red wine has been known to work better on us than a bottle of Ambien. We are not suggesting that you take a bottle of Ambien, but how about a cup of tea or some low-cal hot chocolate or even just a glass of sparkling water with a splash of juice? Many times when we think we need to eat, we're really just thirsty. Sip on something fun and crunch on the ice if your mouth feels like it needs something to do in the middle of the night. Or you could just unbutton your man's pants and occupy your mouth that way.

T - Think About Tomorrow

Have any of you ever eaten something crappy late at night and then woken up in the morning feeling guilty and full or with some sort of gross indigestion? We think you probably have, and we're not ashamed to say that we've totally done this on more than a few occasions. And every time we woke up still tasting the nachos we ate at 2 a.m., we felt like total shit.

The solution to this problem is simple, ladies - just think. Think about how you'll feel in the morning if you start digging through that entire bag of spicy chex mix. We promise that you won't feel nearly as hot as you would if you ate a peach or some other pretty food that comes from our Earth. Trust us; you will have a better day tomorrow if you end today eating like a Hot Chick.

Eating Around The Issue:

There are many reasons that men have an easier time keeping weight off than us girls. Most of them are biological, and so we're not gonna go there right now, but a lot of it also has to do with how they handle their cravings.

Often, when we girls crave some chocolate, we try and deny it. Instead, we use those stupid avoidance tricks from girly magazines. (Sorry, we love girly magazines, but you know what we mean.) We take a walk, and then we eat a bunch of chocolate-flavored rice cakes, thinking they might satisfy us for only about 100 calories. Obviously, it doesn't work.

Now we're full and we're still craving chocolate, so we eat a packet of sugar-free hot chocolate powder for another 50 calories. This only spurns us on. Now, feeling like a pathetic, disgusting, LSE pig, we finally cave in and attack a pint of chocolate ice cream, or a giant box of chocolate-chip cookies. We've now consumed about 1,000 calories, and go to bed hating ourselves. That's not hot.*

Just this once, let's borrow a page from the boys. When they want some chocolate, they don't stress out or torture themselves about it. You won't ever hear them kvetching to their buddies, "Man! I'm craving chocolate like crazy! I don't know what to do about it! I'm such a fat pig!" No - instead, they will relish their craving, and excitedly hit the candy jar or the vending machine, and pick out their favorite morsel. They'll nip it in the bud for maybe a maximum of 200 calories, and their self-worth won't be compromised as a result. This is how Hot Chicks should do it. When we eat something that should be ENJOYABLE, like chocolate, we should ENJOY it. We know, it sounds simple, and it should be.

Chapter 4
How to Hydrate Like a Hot Chick All day Long

Okay girls, it's time to turn on your pretty little brains and use some common sense - you know that it's not hot to gulp down a whole lot of calories that will only end up being drained out of your system before the taste has even left your mouth. It's actually really easy to end up drinking a LOT more calories than you realize - a glass of OJ with breakfast, a cup of sweet tea from your friend's southern mom and a couple of good, old-fashioned wine coolers adds up to about 600 calories. That's about half of what a Hot Chick should really be consuming throughout an entire day! We're not saying that you have to drink boring Diet drinks all day long, but if you pay attention and follow our rules, you'll be hydrated, happy and hot in no time.

Water!

Okay ladies...every diet book since the dawn of "the diet" talks about the importance of water. Well, they are right. Even Atkins got this part correct! Anyway, H2O is our friend. It helps our hair, skin, and nails stay hot and all of our internal organs function properly. Plus, it curbs your appetite, and helps push all those giant pounds of spinach (or chocolate bars) through your digestive system.

Face it girls, it's really hard to feel hot when you're constipated, so drink up. The more you flush your system out and eliminate the toxins, the better you will feel, and the better you feel, the hotter you will look!

We like to frantically, spastically, and/or manically drink water all day long. We always have a bottle of water with us, and about 40 extras rolling around in the back seat of our car. Oh, and no need to count out 6-8 8oz servings — that's not fun and NOT hot. Just pound some water in the morning, drink a giant bottle throughout the day, and then pound some more before bed. If you're not used to drinking so much, no worries - you'll totally get used to it and all those extra trips to the bathroom burn calories!

We think water is delicious, but we know that some of you think it's boring. Okay. Fine. Here are some ways to liven it up like crazy. Try some of these water works and pretty soon you'll be drinking the stuff like it's... water. (Bad joke, sorry!)

Water Works #1 - Make It Fruity

Add a splash of juice to your H20 and you'll get a ton of flavor, a few vitamins, and way fewer calories than a straight glass of the sticky stuff. Or, if you really can't stand the idea of drinking water, think of it as just watering down your juice! It's a glass half full kind of thing.

Water Works #2 - Get Fizzy With It

Seltzer is just as good for you as boring, flat water, but way more exciting! Not only is it as effervescent as your newly confident, completely un-LSE* personality, but it also comes in all sorts of delicious flavors. Start drinking this stuff when you're craving something sweet to sip on, and soon you'll be feeling bubblier than ever!

Water Works #3 - Lemon-Aid

Those bottled and powdered lemonades that you can find in the supermarket are definitely NOT what God intended when he gave us lemons. They're full of sugar and chemicals and all kinds of other grossness. But try making lemonade the Hot Chicks way - just add lemon juice (fresh or bottled, we're not gonna be too picky) and Splenda to your water. It tastes great and has NO calories at all! You just can't beat that. (Don't try.)

Water Works #4 - Freshen Up

Have you seen these new bottled mint waters? They taste pretty good, but they're really just the latest way that some corporate jackass is trying to make money by selling you fancy bottles of water. You'll save about $2 a bottle by adding a simple little mint leaf to your plain or sparkling water, plus you'll always be minty fresh and ready to get some kisses!

Water Works #5 - Just Eat It

When all else fails, you can get your water by just eating a fuckload of watermelon! Did you know that watermelon is 97% water?! Can you believe that? It also has very few calories and tastes awesome. Just be sure to spit those pits out carefully into an embroidered napkin (and not against a closed car window) like the dainty little Hot Chick that you are.

Soda, Pop, Soda-Pop, Or Whatever The Hell YOU Call It

If you down sugary, corn-syrupy, sodium-filled aluminum cans of carbonated nonsense, we are now going to try to talk you out of it. Why mindlessly drink 200 pure empty calories when you can drink something else, and then eat those 200 calories in the form of chocolate and/or cheese? Soda is just not good for you, and you know that, so stop it. Unless, of course, a can of Dr. Pepper to YOU is like a bag of M&M's to US. Then, by all means, go ahead and pop open a can every now and then. *(NOTE: "now and then" does NOT mean "every day.")*

We *are* however giant fans of *diet* drinks. We try not to have them too often, but we admit that we are kind of addicted to Diet Coke. *(NOTE: "kind of" does mean "extremely").* Yeah, yeah, it *may* cause cancer, but it has ZERO calories, and it just makes us happy - and when we are happy, we are hot! We recently discovered the Splenda-sweetened Diet Hansen's, which have no sodium, no calories, no aspartame, and no caffeine. Obviously, it's not quite as much fun as Diet Coke, but we're getting used to it.

Juice

We don't drink juice. It's so full of sugar that it's downright sticky, and it's totally not hot to ingest anything sticky, ladies (unless you're in love). Anyway, we don't care if it's all natural juice with no added sugars, either. Yes, sugar is natural, but it also makes us fat. Sorry, but it's true. We've just learned that it's soooooooooo much better for us to eat a freaking orange and chase it with a ton of water than it is to suck down 300 calories of sugary orange pulp from a carton.

It doesn't matter if it's freshly squeezed, concentrated or canned - calorie for calorie, it's simply better to just eat the fruit you crave instead of drinking it. And please don't bother with those "juice drink" things. Break out your reading glasses and actually look at the ingredients. They admit it right there on the label—the stuff only has 10% juice, at best! That means the other 90% of this stuff is sugar, sugar, and some more sugar. We'd rather consume our sugar by eating a piece of chocolate cake than from sucking down grape-flavored liquid, but that's just us.

What Not To Drink

Some of these are obvious (at least we hope so!) but here's a list of beverages that a Hot Chick should never, ever drink:

Drink Don't #1 - Smoothies

No. Stop. Don't. That GIANT cup of creamy, fruity slush has more sugar in it than our giant bag of bulk candy. Adding a scoop of protein, fat-burner, or extra vitamin C doesn't make it any better. Trust us, you'll look hotter holding a pretty peach than you will sucking on a Styrofoam bucket that will only leave you famished shortly after you pee it out.

Drink Don't #2 - Vitamin/Fruit Waters

Read these labels very carefully. They actually have a ton of sugar in them, and are also totally unnecessary. Water is good for you the way nature made it, okay? You don't need to add in vitamins and a whole lot of calories along with them!

Drink Don't #3 - Powdered Drinks

Any powder sitting that's on your shelves right now may have the *potential* to become a beverage, but that doesn't mean that you should drink it! This stuff is bad for you and really doesn't taste very good, either. The same thing goes for pre-sweetened teas and any other bottles of sugary bullshit. You'll definitely use less sugar if it's up to you to add it yourself, and you'll even burn a few calories by stirring!

Drink Don't #4 – "All Natural" Sodas

Let us repeat this again – SUGAR IS ALL NATURAL! But that doesn't mean that we can ingest buckets of sugar all day long if we want to feel and look hot! These cans of natural carbonation are full of the stuff, and sometimes they have even more calories than regular Coke! Buy diet natural sodas or just start drinking flavored seltzer, stop whining and learn to love it.

Drink Don't #5 – Egg Creams

If we have to tell you why it's not hot to drink something with both the words "egg" AND "cream" in the title, then we're obviously not doing a good job! Egg creams basically consist of a bunch of half and half with a cup of chocolate syrup mixed in. Save these weird beverages for very, very special occasions like when you're in the 1950's and you go on a date at the local soda fountain. That's really the only appropriate time to drink them.

Drink Don't #6 – Pina Coladas

Hey, you're smart, and we know that you already know that these creamy bastions of deliciousness are kinda fattening. Well, you're wrong. They're not "kinda" anything. They are seriously, critically and acutely fucked up*. These drinks have about 1,000 calories EACH, and the last thing any girl needs to do is suck down an entire day's worth of calories one after another while wearing A BIKINI!! This is sure to make you feel like a proverbial beached whale, and guess what? That's not hot. Try your best to stay away from them in most instances, but if you're in Puerto Rico with your boyfriend or on your honeymoon in Aruba and you want to treat yourself just this once, go ahead. On those occasions (and those occasions only), the memory of that drink will actually be worth it.

Chapter 5
How to Eat Like a Hot Chick
At Dinner

When you're trying to feel hot, dinner is often just a reenactment of lunch, not some giant meal with every single food group, like some so-called diet books would have you believe. Simply put - a meat, a vegetable and a starch just add up to too many calories for us to consume every night of the week. That doesn't mean that we skimp on nutrients or starve ourselves like a couple of Mary Kates* - quite the opposite.

You just need to reconsider how you define a "meal." You do not need a giant slab of meat just because it is dinnertime, nor do you need calorie-packed side dishes or more than one course. Those are for special occasions. For every day, your dinner should be simple, filling and light. We promise that if you start following our Hot Chick's advice at dinner, you'll end up going to bed feeling much, much hotter in your nightie, and that's what this is all about.

Dinner Don'ts

There are many ways to screw up dinner so that you won't feel like a Hot Chick. Most of them should be pretty obvious to you by this point. We're not gonna reiterate that you shouldn't order a whole meatball pizza and a bucket of hot wings, but we do need to address a couple of very common, terrible mistakes that many women make.

Dinner Don't #1 - Frozen Faux Pas

We feel that the worst possible thing that you could do at the end of a long, hard day is a open up a freezing cold box, pull out a small tray of food covered in ice crystals that have been settling there for months, zap it with micro waves, and then call that dinner. That's not dinner! That's just disgusting! All frozen meals are full of hundreds of weird chemicals and ingredients that end with "xanthian." Sorry, but we like our food to come from a farmer, butcher or baker, not a chemistry set.

This stuff is not made for a Hot Chick's body and it's not good for any body. Go ahead and feed them to your dog for a week and just see what happens. We are in no way supporting cruelty to animals, we're just sure that even your cute little puppy will realize that they taste like cat shit and would rather starve than lick pasty, sticky sauce off of plastic. Oh, and have you looked at the sodium content? The amount of salt in just 6 inches of frozen food is enough to keep a shark alive and swimming in your freezer for years!

There is nothing good about eating a frozen meal. And we don't care if you buy the "healthy" versions that are zone friendly and only have 300 calories. If you want to eat a 300 calorie bullshit dinner that will leave you feeling famished just an hour later, eat 4 pieces of See's Candy. At least it'll taste good and you'll have some variety, because all frozen meals taste EXACTLY the same. The chicken tastes just like the pasta, and the beef tastes just like the broccoli. That is just freaking weird, man. And if you're into eating weird things for dinner, try hummus in a bowl of oatmeal. You'll be way hotter. The bottom line is, do not eat frozen dinners, ever! Unless you are an astronaut or live in an igloo; then we'll let it slide.

Dinner Don't #2 - Take Me Out

It is so incredibly easy to pick up a pizza, a bucket of chicken, or zillions of tiny white cardboard containers on your way home from work. We know. It requires little thought, and even less work. But here's the thing - this stuff is not good for you. It is laden with fat, calories, preservatives and cornstarch, and will eventually make you feel like crap. Plus, we always eat more of it than we planned. There are all sorts of justifications for this, such as, "It won't taste as good tomorrow anyway, so why waste it?" We're sure you've come up with more clever excuses than that, but no matter what, this always causes us to end our day feeling bloated, unsatisfied, and totally LSE*.

We say, save these foods for when you really want them—when you choose to go out for Chinese, or you find yourself at a picnic and simply MUST try the fried chicken. Taking this stuff out or ordering it in on a regular basis is also expensive. Why pay all that money for restaurant food to just eat it on your couch alone? And is it really that much quicker to order in than it is to prepare something simple? No. Does it really taste that much better? Well, maybe, to be honest, but sometimes we have to sacrifice taste to be really hot.

Dinner Do's

Some healthy, simple every day meals can totally be fun, though. So throw out those lame Lean Cuisines and pay attention! These dinner ideas are easy, cheap and will leave you feeling super sexy for any and all post dinner activities that you can think of.

Dinner Delite # 1 - Hunt And Gather

One of our favorite dinners is a picnic that we eat in our very own home. It's called the hunter-gatherer meal, and it consists of a giant salad, some toasty bread, cheese and fruit. We've even found that if we arrange it all cute on a plate and add a small meat supplement for him, our boyfriend loves this meal, too! Open a bottle of wine, spread out on the floor, and you'll feel as sexy as if you two were eating in a little European bistro. Just clear the dishes off the floor before you start getting *too* hot, though. Chunks of ceramic in your butt aren't very hot.

Dinner Delite #2 - Go Fish

Fish is another great dinner that you can easily make at home. And please stop worrying that your apartment is gonna stink like fish for the rest of your life if you cook it. That will only happen if you either buy fish that's rank to begin with or you really fuck it up. Make sure you trust your fish source and don't buy it too far ahead of time. We know how much it blows to have to battle the supermarket lines right after work.

That can totally give us a horrible case of OWL Syndrome*, but it's still a lot better than having to sniff your fish curiously for an hour before cooking it.

A lot of recipes tell you to smother fish in butter and oil before cooking it, but that's totally unnecessary and obviously not hot. We're sure you've heard by now that fish has lots of good fats and natural oils. (That's where the term "fish oils" comes from.) All you have to do is drizzle a little bit of olive oil on the fish. (Measure it out, okay? One teaspoon per piece of fish.) Then throw that sucker under the broiler for like 10 minutes and voila! You cooked fish! Squeeze some lemon juice on there and your roommates will be super impressed. Try this on a date or even by yourself one weeknight. It's so much healthier than takeout, plus it'll spare you having to put up with the delivery guy hitting on you because you're so hot.

Fish can make a fun little fiesta too, girls! Try throwing some in your George Foreman Grill and then folding it into a healthy tortilla. Add some salsa and either a bit of cheese or a few slices of avocado, and you have a hot little grilled fish taco. Invite your friends over and make Taco Tuesday! This may sound kind of dorky to you now, but after one of these tacos, a Corona Light and a shot of tequila, you'll feel so hot you'll want to suck on more than just a lime!

Dinner Delite #3 - Stir It Up

If you're a vegetarian or eat in a lot of Chinese restaurants, you're probably very familiar with the concept of a stir fry.

But when you order them out or in they tend to have been "stirred" and "fried" in a whole lot of oil and doused with a bunch of equally fucked up* sauces. Well, don't worry, because we have perfected the hottest, leanest stir fry ever. We go to the local farmers' market and load up on every veggie that we can manage to carry. (This also makes for a very good workout and then we can skip butt class* to cook.)

Zucchini is especially good, but add broccoli, onions, peppers - literally every single veggie that you like (and even some that you think you don't). Then we go home and chop up all of our veggies, and heat up a pan that we've sprayed with a bunch of Pam. See, stir fries actually don't need any oil at all! If you really love the taste of olive oil, you can put ONE tablespoon into the pan, but that's it. Flip everything around in there while it cooks, and when it's done, throw on some soy or teriyaki sauce (both of which have very few calories) or even just some lemon juice and a TINY bit more olive oil.

This meal is great because you can eat a ton of it and it has basically no calories. But it *does* have a ton of vitamins that will make every pore on your body a little bit hotter. This is a great dinner on days when you've eaten a somewhat hearty lunch (like pizza or some giant, delicious sandwich).

Of course, feel free to add in some chicken or tofu or even a small amount of another lean meat if you want, but please don't live in fear of becoming a protein deficient Mary Kate* just because you ate one meal without it. If you bought this book, it's practically impossible for you to be protein deficient (but check with your doctor first, please, so that we don't get sued).

Dinner Delite # 4 - A Taste Of Italy

If you had a light lunch or are totally PMSie, there is often nothing more satisfying than a warm, steaming plate of pasta or a cheesy pizza for dinner. And here's the good news! We are here to give you permission to say fuck you to those who think Italian food is fattening. Go to Italy and check out the women. They are *all* hot! And do you think they are eating Atkin's bars for lunch and frozen meals for dinner? Nope. They're not. They are eating yummy, comforting, reasonably portioned Italian food every freaking night.

When we want a taste of Italy for dinner and don't have time to simmer a sauce for 4 hours, we use these cheap, healthy, low-cal tricks for curbing that craving for Italian. (FYI: These are especially fun to make on Sunday nights as you curl up with that boy who twitterpates* you and watch the Soprano's.)

Italian Invention a) Fake Fettuccini

Take what ever pasta noodle you prefer (we suggest whole wheat), measure out a serving, boil water, and cook them to your liking. After you have drained the water, throw the pasta back into that hot pan, add some I Can't Believe It's Not Butter, a tad bit of milk, a dash of garlic powder, some salt and a fuckton of parmesan cheese. Viola! Your mouth will be so happy, and your hips will not hate you.

Italian Invention b) Pretend Parmesan

If you don't know how to cook a quick marinara sauce, you better learn because this is totally impressive to the boys. We know that there are actually many fast ways to a man's heart, but his stomach is always a good one. Anyway, if you can't make a fresh sauce, you should learn, but in the meantime, just buy a bottled tomato sauce that you like, but make sure you read the labels for fat and sodium content. Then, slice up an eggplant or take a chicken breast, throw them on a George Foreman Grill (see below for more on this hot invention), and cook until tender and juicy. Cover the eggplant or chicken with parmesan cheese, hot tomato sauce and then more parmesan cheese. Look at that, ladies! You made quick, healthy eggplant/chicken parmesan. That is definitely delightful!

Italian Invention c) Practically Pizza

There are a couple ways for you to do this, and both are much better for your bod than delivery. Take a slice of whole wheat healthy bread, spread on some sauce, tomato, basil and a bit of low fat mozzarella. Cover it with another slice of that healthy bread and then put it in your George Foreman Grill. When you open the lid you will have a perfect pizza Panini! Or, get a healthy, low fat tortilla, add sauce, cheese, veggies, etc., and then just broil it in the oven for a few minutes. There you have it, another Hot Chick way to enjoy pizza without adding cellulite to your new ass.

Dinner Delite # 5 - Hot Potato

Baked potatoes were a big diet food in the 80's. Those hot ass dancers that wore half-tops in Flashdance were totally eating baked potatoes for dinner. So we say put your hair in a side ponytail, cut up a t-shirt, throw on some leg warmers and eat a hot potato. Just wash it, poke it with a fork a bunch of times like it's a voodoo doll of your ex, and put it in the oven for an hour.

Now here's the fun part - add a bunch of fun shit to it! I Can't Believe It's Not Butter, a few veggies, maybe a couple pieces of lean protein, and then cover it in a bit of melty cheese. We like to do this with sweet potatoes too! Don't let the name fool you - sweet potatoes are actually even healthier than the regular white ones. They have more fiber and are filled with the same anti-aging, eye brightening vitamins that carrots have! How hot is that?

NOTE: If you have never heard of George Foreman's Lean, Mean, Fat-Reducing Grilling Machine, we're pretty sure you have been living in a cave somewhere. The Foreman Grill is fucking awesome! We wish we invented it or just slapped our names on it like he did, because that guy is like a bazilionairre now. It's only like $40, you can cook anything and everything on it, and you can watch all the extra fat drip off your food and into a cute little fat-catching tray.

(Sometimes, when we're feeling really gross, we have destructive fantasy sequences about what would happen if we tried to grill our own thigh. How much crap would get squished out and dumped into the fat catching tray? Please don't try that at home.)*

Anyway, the grill rocks! You can grill chicken, fish, steak, any kind of veggie and make all sorts of fun grilled sandwiches. We don't know George, but we say go out and get one of his grills. It's a hot little item to have in your kitchen!

A Note On Vegetarians:

We think that women who want to help save the animals and the planet by only eating food from our mama earth are definitely eating like Hot Chicks. We think you are awesome for being selective about what you put into your hot-ass body. HOWEVER, we have a giant pet peeve about girls who call themselves "vegetarians," but really eat a bunch of meaty bullshit and talk a bunch of bullshit.

Now pay attention - a vegetarian is a person who does not eat meat. Period. This might seem really obvious, but we actually know many girls who call themselves vegetarians but will eat steak at a bbq and say shit like, "Cook mine really well-done, 'cause I'm a vegetarian." What the fuck? Correct us if we're wrong, but the last time we checked, burning meat does not magically turn it into a vegetable.

We also hate hearing crap like, "It's not my fault that I'm 25 pounds overweight, because I'm a vegetarian and the only thing for me to eat every night is Pizza Hut." That's bullshit. Even if you are one of the few vegetarians who doesn't care about being healthy and you really just love animals, you still want to be a Hot Chick, right? Making excuses for not looking your best is NOT hot, so forget it. Start eating, um...we don't know... VEGETABLES, and those 25 pounds will melt away like cheese on your boyfriend's double burger.

Now, if you are truly a vegan or a vegetarian, please remember to be kind. Not everyone shares your discipline and values, *and that's okay! You don't want some BMS*, vegetarian guy, right? So please do not talk shit to those who eat meat. Don't look down on your friend's turkey sandwich and say things like, "Eeewwww! Gross! How can you eat that?" Let them eat whatever they want - you don't want them to say that shit about your tofu, do you? So play fair. You are not better than them. You are just different. And different is hot, but ego is not.*

Chapter 6
How to Party Like a Hot Chick

For those of us who are over 21, this might be one of the most important sections of the book. So often we gals will kill ourselves at butt class* and eat apples and salads all week so that we can squeeze into those magic* jeans on Friday night. Then, without even realizing it, we end up consuming a Thanksgiving dinner's worth of calories in the first hour at the bar. This leaves us bloated and angry well into the next week. Sound familiar? Well, don't panic. We can help.

Don't worry, we are NOT going to tell you to sip on a glass of Diet 7-up with lime and see how much fun it is to *pretend* that you're drunk. That's playing small*, which is not hot at all. Remember that the #1 way to look like a Hot Chick is to have FUN. It's our heyday* and we're young and fun and LOVE to party, socialize, and have a good time. That's why it was crucial for us to come up with a foolproof plan that allows us to enjoy ourselves like the rest of the world without expanding our waistlines. Follow our simple secrets, and we will keep you looking and feeling hot until last call - or, even better, the morning after.

Mixing Mistakes

Let's face it - we Hot Chicks love all those girly mixed drinks. Margaritas, Pina Coladas, Mudslides, Mojitos, and Apple Martinis all look really pretty and fun and taste like candy. That's the problem - they pretty much *are* candy. Each one of those cocktails is loaded with sugary nonsense and tons of sodium and can run anywhere from 400 to 1,200 calories EACH! And be honest, how many times do we go out and only have ONE drink?

We notice that the crazier and more colorful our cocktails get, the less hot we feel in our tank tops and short skirts as we try to get comfortable on that barstool. It's not actually the *alcohol* that makes these drinks do about the same damage as cheesecake. It's all the crap they *add* to the alcohol to make it taste sweet.

Vodka, Gin, Tequila, and even some of the clearer Rums only have about 70-80 calories a shot. It's the pre-made mixes and colas and tonic and concentrated fruit juices and creamy flavorings they add to the shots that turn these cocktails into giant calorie fests. Remember that the clever names of those mixed drinks are actually vicious lies. "Sex on the beach" should more accurately be called, "Chubby mixed drink guzzler sitting alone on the beach in a control top one-piece."

But have no fear. If mixed drinks are what you fancy, then follow our oh-so-clever bar codes, and we promise that you'll have just as much fun, get just as tipsy, and feel so much hotter when that semi-cute guy is trying to get you to go home with him.

Bar Code #1 - Take Out The Tonic

A lot of smart girls don't know this, but tonic actually has the same amount of calories as regular old cola. Seriously. And it doesn't even have much taste, so it's totally not worth it. Add plain *Soda Water* to your favorite gin or vodka instead, and ask for a ton of limes. It's refreshing, will make you happy, and you save about 150 calories per drink. One of our favorite new summer cocktails is rum and soda water. Try this one at your next sweltering August happy hour, and you'll get buzzed and hydrated at the same time! And if you girls need it sweet, remember to always stash some splenda in that little black purse of yours.

Bar Code #2 - Forget Flavors!

Exchange your coconut rum with coke for Bicardi and diet, and you'll save an easy 180 calories - calories that we promise will taste better in the form of hangover food, but we'll get to that later.

Bar Code #3 - Lose The Juice

We know it's hard to believe, but six ounces of cranberry juice mixed with your orange flavored vodka creates a drink that easily has 250 calories. Try having plain vodka with soda water and a SPLASH of your favorite juice. We promise you won't feel deprived.

Bar Code #4 - Get Creative!

Figure out how to make a lower calorie version of your favorite drink. When we want a margarita, but also want to feel as hot as possible in that new bra and panty set, we ask for tequila on the rocks with a SPLASH of triple-sec, lots of fresh squeezed lime juice, and a tiny bit of salt. No, of course it's not as good! But we'd rather eat a giant bowl of guacamole than drink 350 calories worth of sweet & sour mix.

Bar Code #5 - Straight Is Sexy!

Okay, this is possibly our penultimate Hot Chicks drink secret. Try drinking like *we* drink, and remove the mixers completely! It may take a few rough weekends to get used to it, but try sipping on a Vodka Martini, and remember to eat the olives for a perfect mini midnight snack. If you have bad memories of vodka, go ahead and order *your* favorite hard alcohol on the rocks. We promise that if there are any guys at the bar who aren't totally intimidated by your fabulousness, they will be begging for your phone number.

Shooting Successfully

If you can keep it together and still feel hot after taking shots at the bar, then we give you mad props. Our philosophy is to just do ONE shot per night out on the town. Go ahead and have a birthday shot, or a shot to drown your break-up blues, but any more than that and you might be asking for trouble.

FYI: All the same bar codes apply to shots. The formula is easy - the crazier the name, the more crap that shot or drink has added to it. We'd rather skip the "Surfer on Acid," and consume a 200-calorie ounce of chocolate.

Water Or Wasted!!

We need to pause for a moment here and stress something very important - a sloppy, crazy, pukey, slutty, LSE* emotional drunk chick is *not* a Hot Chick! Please don't be that annoying girl at the party. Have a good time, but PLEASE, PLEASE, PLEASE keep it together!!

Two things can help you not make a fool of yourself: common sense and H2O. Have a drink, then grab a bottle of water and mingle for a while. Then go ahead and do a shot, but chase it with some water.

Match each drink with a few ounces of water, and you will stay in the perfect tipsy zone all night. And if you know you're going to be out from 7 p.m. to 1 a.m., don't have 4 drinks in the first hour. Hot Chicks are smart chicks. Use that pretty little head and come up with a plan, or you might accidentally wake up somewhere really weird next to someone even weirder.

Beer Blunders

Maybe you're in college, or perhaps you just found yourself at a barbeque or a beach party or a whiffle ball game, or maybe (just maybe) you really adore the taste of ale. Personally, we're not huge fans of how bloated those wheaty bubbles make us feel. Plus, we're not too keen on having to run to the ladies room every half hour (though it does give us a good opportunity to reapply our lip gloss).

But even though beer isn't our drink of choice, we understand how common it is, how cheap it is, and how good it feels on those glossed lips on a hot summer day, or after a hard day at work. Our rules on beer are simple and easy to follow, and you'll end up feeling just like one of the guys (but obviously way hotter).

Beer Law #1 – Believe What You See!

All of those commercials and billboards that glamorize low-carb/light beers are not false advertising. Each light beer has 30-50 less calories than a regular dark beer. Just make this easy switch, and help prevent a possible beer belly.

Beer Law #2 – Don't Forget How To Count

This rule actually applies to all alcoholic drinks, but we think you should definitely keep track of the number of beers you throw down. We just think that chicks might be a bit hotter *with* a six-pack than they are *chugging* a six-pack.

Beer Law #3 - Let The Boys Be Boys

Yes, guys like chicks they can watch the game and crack open a beer with, but there is no reason for you to try to keep up with them. We think that a girl who drinks too many beers with the guys is kind of like the guy who's a little bit too willing to go shoe shopping. It's just a bit suspicious. Trust us, if you have 1 beer for your man's every 3, you'll feel way hotter and be just as cool. We promise.

Beer Law #4 - Beer Before Liquor, Never Been Sicker...

This quote is just noteworthy. Some women can stay really, really hot after shotgunning a Corona and then chasing it down with a Godiva Chocolate Martini. For a lot of us, though, this is a recipe for disaster, and we find ourselves hugging the porcelain late at night instead of a hot guy.

NOTE: There are these things called "beer goggles," and everyone has a pair. Beer Goggles are invisible glasses that magically go on after someone has consumed approximately 1-4 drinks, and they make everyone else look way, way hotter. If you are having a gross day of PMS, and you're freaked about going out to see that crush of yours, stay in and watch a Sex & the City re-run, and then go out LATER. Give that guy time to have a couple beers.

It's weird how it works, but you will feel so much sexier just knowing that he is wearing his beer goggles. However, these magic glasses can also work against us. Beer goggles can get foggy, and we magically* don ours after exactly 1½ martinis and become very heydayish*. This can be dangerous and sometimes we end up flirting (or worse, but we won't talk about that here) with a dude that is just not up to our standards, so beware.*

We also want to take this opportunity to warn you about another kind of goggles, called "Job Goggles." If you're bored at work all day, co-workers slowly start appearing more and more attractive. This has nothing to do with food, but just be aware of it before you start making out with the office boy at your next company holiday party.

The Ways To Wine

Wine has possibly been around since beginning of time. Go read that old mythology textbook, and find out about Dionysus and the Bacchae, and all of their crazy parties. Wine was all they needed to have fun, and it's still a staple in many countries, cultures and religions. Many people believe that a glass of wine a day can keep the doctor away, and this antioxidant filled treat is made from grapes, for crying out loud! It's gotta be good for us, right?

Well, we've been sipping on wine since childhood, and have come to realize that if we are not feeling hot after an evening of vino, it's usually just because we also consumed 12,000 calories worth of cheese and crackers. There aren't too many ways to screw up with wine, but we do have some important info for you that will keep you from *whining* about your waist.

Wine Rule #1 - The Redder The Better

Dry red wine, like merlot and some cabernets, have the least amount of calories and sugar of any wine, and they're supposed to be better for our hearts. But pay attention, because depending how big your glass is, you're looking at 70 to 100 calories every time that cute sommelier tops it off.

Wine Rule #2 - Don't Destroy Dinner

Sometimes something really unfortunate happens when we have a bottle of wine with a meal - we end up eating like we've been out chopping wood all day instead of lying out by the pool. Be aware of how many glasses you're actually pouring, and equally vigilant about how many times you ask the waiter to re-fill your breadbasket.

Wine Rule #3 - Add It To The Grocery List!

We cannot overstate the importance of having wine in your house! Some of you might not agree, but we think that all Hot Chicks should have a bottle of white in the fridge and at least one of red in the cupboard. Let's face it, you never know when an old passionate flame is gonna blow through town, or when you're going to end up in your apartment with a cute new guy who swears he's just gonna crash on your couch. In either of these cases, a glass of vino will make everyone involved look and feel hotter.

Celebrating with Champagne

Champagne has about the same amount of calories as wine, but that's not our point here. This stuff is dangerous. Champagne is like that guy who you keep sleeping with despite the red flags* just because you're so twitterpated*. We have learned our lesson (over and over again) with those tall pretty glasses of bubbles.

Champagne sneaks up on you just when you least expect it. It's so glamorous, and it goes down so easily, but trust us when we tell you that it's *not hot at all* when it comes back up. Have one less glass than you think you deserve, and be sure to eat something more solid than a frozen yogurt cake before you start toasting.

What To Eat, When To Eat, And Why You Must Eat...

Some women don't realize just how very important *food* is when it comes to alcohol. What you do or don't eat can make the difference between puking your guts out alone in a cab or making out with that guy you've been having fantasy sequences* about - the difference between showing up at the office on Monday with that after sex glow, and walking in with hot flashes and 10 pounds of bloat on your face. Yes, it's *that* serious.

And this is one of those cases where we can't take clues from the clueless boys. The male body was apparently built to handle beer bongs and Long Island Ice Teas on an empty stomach, followed by 4 death dogs (that mystery meat they sell on the street) swallowed whole at 4 a.m. Please understand that in order for us to stay looking and feeling hot in a night of drinking, it's crucial for us to precisely plan out our food.

Before The Bar

We totally understand that sometimes there just isn't enough time sit down and eat a real meal before you head out for a cocktail. Maybe you're going straight from the office to happy hour, or maybe you're too nervous because that fantasy sequence* guy might be there. Whatever your excuse is, it's no excuse, so stop apologizing for yourself and playing small*.

We Hot Chicks are in control of our lives, and so we need to work it out. If you start a night of drinking on an empty stomach, there is a very good chance that you are going to get too drunk too fast, and end up puking in your purse. Either that or you'll become that dreaded emotionally unstable chick who can't handle her alcohol and ends up crying in the corner.

Eat something balanced and solid *before* you go out! Something that will stick to your ribs, not some iceberg lettuce and fat free ranch or a giant bowl of M&M's. Maybe have that slice of pizza you've been craving, or order in some healthy Chinese food and pick at it while you're curling you hair. Whatever you do, make sure you've consumed something you can at least call a "mini- meal" before you say "cheers." It will save you from sickness and/or pigging out at the appetizer table.

At The Party

So if you've done what we've said and eaten something *before* you arrived at your drinking destination, then you shouldn't be tempted to eat anything else, right? Hardly. We need to start this off by reminding you that alcohol lowers your ability to make good judgments. Forget about those one or two guys that you shouldn't have gone home with – that's a different book. Alcohol actually lowers our blood sugar, not to mention our willpower, and so we're far more susceptible when it comes to party food. When we get too tipsy, we suddenly have the capability to eat *all* the potato salad at the barbecue, or we end up asking the bartender to refill or p-nut pretzel bowl nine times.

We know how much fun it is to eat when we're drinking, but think about how much hotter you'll feel the next day if you manage to control yourself. Go ahead and have a few chips and salsa with that Amstel Light, but keep it together! We'd rather you end up with prince charming in your cleavage then sprinkles and crumbs falling out of your bra.

After Last Call

If you had some salmon and brown rice at 6 p.m. and then 2 martinis, a glass of champagne, half of a Bacardi and diet and you're still walking and talking like a Hot Chick, a 2 a.m. snack might be necessary in order to save you from feeling like complete crap in the morning. Again, it can be really hard to not eat like a ravenous shark when you're intoxicated, but another little mini-meal after your cocktails can help stop the spinning and put you to sleep, all while diminishing the possibility of a nasty hangover.

Go ahead and go with your friends to that 24-hour diner, but try really hard to make a smart choice. Also, we hot, smart, busy chicks aren't partying every night, so on these special occasions, we think this is a fine time for that bagel or pizza, or a little bit of cheesy nonsense. Grease is known to absorb some of the alcohol in your system, so go ahead and have some French fries, but just remember to watch your portions, and know that tomorrow night you might want to eat a pound of spinach for dinner.

Hangover Help

If you wake on Sunday morning with a horrible hangover, you probably didn't follow any of our suggestions. But that's okay. It's your heyday* and Hot Chicks are not perfect. You may be too nauseas to even think about food, or else you may wake up hungrier than EVER! Whatever the case, we can't overstress the importance of WATER.

Alcohol dehydrates you, so drinking a gallon of water the day after partying is essential to help keep you hot. Also, as horrible as it may sound, EXERCISE is a must. Just go sweat for an hour (any way you like) and we promise that you'll be happy you did.

As far a food goes, if you didn't have onion rings and a strawberry shake after last call, then treat yourself to a nice satisfying cheesy/greasy brunch and pop a couple of Advil. Or if you didn't eat all of the birthday cake the night before, then this is a good time for those chocolate chip pancakes. But remember, in order to not completely hate yourself on Monday morning, you're gonna have to get it together and eat a giant bowl of steamed veggies for dinner.

Note: We are trying really hard to stick to the subject and not kick your butt about drunk driving and condoms. But just remember that if you're smart and respect yourself, you're hot. So please get yourself home in one piece, and always remember to protect yourself if you're gonna get a piece.

Chapter 7
How to Eat Out Like a Hot Chick
At a Restaurant

If you took a little trip to the kitchens of some of your favorite restaurants, you would get an instant case of OWL Syndrome* just by looking at the amount of oil, butter and lard (yes, *lard*) that they use in everything, even the healthiest stuff on the menu! Yes, it tastes better than the stuff you make at home, and there's a very good and simple reason for that - because you would never *dream* of using all of that nonsense without waking up screaming in absolute horror! It is like a self destructive fantasy sequence* happening in real life!

You have to be very, very, very careful with what you order in a restaurant, but you also don't want to come across like some picky bitch that says stuff like, "Please don't use a lot of oil on that." They are going to use a lot of oil - that's just what they do. That'd be like asking Mel Gibson not to hate Jews. But ANYWAY, don't worry! It is totally possible to eat out all the time without feeling gross. Just follow these rules and trust us! Because being LSE* and hating yourself isn't hot no matter what you eat.

Menu Meanings

Sometimes things that sound totally benign when written all pretty on a menu end up making you feel gross and miserable and you can't even figure out why! That's because restaurants often have their own secret, trick language that makes things sound way healthier than they really are. We have studied this vernacular, and have translated it for you below. These terms are the keys to not fucking up in a restaurant, so study these words like you have a vocab test on Saturday night.*

Grilled *= Fried in butter and/or oil (Note: When dining at Friendly's or another similar chain establishment, it means Fried in partially hydrogenated nonsense.)*

Marinated *= Sitting in butter and/or oil*

Crusted *= Fried*

Drizzled *(in oil) = Soaked (in oil)*

Sautéed *= Cooked in oil*

Seared *(or **Pan Seared**) = Fried in oil*

Stir-Fried *= Tossed around in oil*

At A Diner

Diners are evil places where the greasier the food is, the better it tastes, and when they try to throw us a bone and put something healthy on the menu it totally doesn't work. This presents a challenge, but we can work it out. First of all, don't order that "health salad" that they always put on the menu just to torture you. Can somebody please tell us what the fuck is up with this concoction? Since when do cottage cheese, cantaloupe and a few slices of mealy tomato make for an acceptable dinner?! And then they throw a giant glob of Jell-O on top, as if that's supposed to help! WTF??

Anyway, there are better choices. Most diners actually have really good Greek salads, and they're pretty good for you. (Just be careful with the olive oil as always, please.) Don't you dare order a chef salad, though, with those giant chunks of cheese and processed meat cubes. That's not cool. Also think about a turkey club, and consider losing one or two of the extra bread layers they inexplicably throw in there.

Diners are diners, though, and sometimes you have to just embrace what they're all about. This is not the time to order seafood and think you're doing yourself a favor. How they can have even remotely fresh seafood at a diner when nobody else has ordered it in 7 years is totally beyond us. Instead, you can have a grilled cheese, skip the bacon, and only eat a FEW of the inevitable fries. Or mix it up and order scrambled eggs for dinner and have a salad tomorrow morning for breakfast! We Hot Chicks are unpredictable, aren't we?

Turning Japanese

We LOVE sushi! It's got more protein than an MTRX shake and it is way more delicious. Plus, have you noticed how hot most Japanese chicks are? That's no coincidence, girls, so pick up those chopsticks!

(Note: chopsticks are a great diet tool and one reason that we think those Asian girls are so thin. If you have a habit of eating too fast, switch to these ancient utensils. They not only slow you down, but also instantly eliminate a lot of bad foods from your diet. No more ice-cream, cheese sauce or porterhouses for you until you learn to lift them with two tiny sticks.)

Anyway, here are the basics on sushi: regular sushi and sashimi are just plain fish that you eat with rice. It's practically impossible to fuck this up; all of the different fishies are yummy and good for you. (We don't think it's hot to worry about mercury poisoning or anything like that, so we choose not to.)

Sushi rolls are our favorite, though. Those genius mixologists behind the sushi bar combine fish with different veggies and sauces and other kinds of fish, and they always taste amazing. Some of these aforementioned sauces are kind of fucked up*, though, so there are definitely certain types of rolls to avoid. Here are our rules for eating them without feeling like you're going to roll yourself home afterwards (haha).

Rolls Rule #1 – Forget The Fried!

Just because sushi is generally healthy, that doesn't mean that you can get away with sticking your handroll in a deep-fryer and calling that dinner! Lots of rolls secretly include pieces of fried fish. Just look out for the lingo – when the description of a roll includes the word "tempura," that's a no-no. Tempura is Japanese for fried. When they mention "tempura flakes" that's no good, either. Tempura flakes are just pieces of fried nonsense stuck in the roll next to your fish. That's like peeling the fried shit off of your Kentucky Fried Chicken and sticking it into a sushi roll. Gross.

Rolls Rule #2 – Cream The Cheese!

Some sushi rolls actually contains cream cheese! Isn't that insane? Let's not kid ourselves, ladies; nobody eats cream cheese in Japan. When you eat cream cheese with salmon, it's called LOX, not sushi. These cream cheese filled tubes are often inexplicably called Philadelphia rolls, but we think that's an insult to our forefathers, so we don't order them.

Rolls Rule #3 – Mayo Mistakes

This is an evil secret of most sushi restaurants – lots of them make their spicy tuna roll with a fuckload of mayonnaise! Isn't that gross? Somehow they bury the mayo in there so that you can barely even notice it, but it's hiding in there, waiting to make us fat. We were so bummed when we learned this, because spicy tuna was previously one of our favorites – but not any more! We're not wasting our expensive, sushi-grade albacore on glorified tuna salad, thank you very much.

Other Options

We know that some of you just don't like the idea of raw fish, kind of like how we feel about the whole dead baby chicken fetus thing. We'd love to change your minds, but there are actually lots of other healthy things to order at Japanese restaurants, so it's no biggie. Miso soup is really good for you thanks to that plankton or whatever's floating around in there, and it has practically no calories, so always order that to start. Another good appy is edamame - eating those straight-up soybeans is like mainlining tofu into your veins. Yum.

Of course you shouldn't order any kind of tempura - whether it's shrimp or beef or vegetable, it's still fried. Skip the noodle dishes, too, which are kinda heavy, and order salmon or chicken teriyaki. Those are both really good choices - just don't go too crazy with the giant bowl of rice they give you. You should also definitely avoid those weird dishes with fried tofu in them. We know you're trying to do a good thing by eating tofu, but if it's fried, forget it.

Mexicana Mama

Here is a little unknown skeleton in the Mexican cupboard - you know that *long* list of complicated dishes on the menu of every Mexican restaurant? Well, it's all exactly the same stuff. Pretty much every dish you can order along with your Margarita consists of meat and cheese rolled up (or on top of) a giant tortilla. None of it is the best for us, so we can't have Mexican food every night, as much as we love our guacamole and those damn Margaritas.

But Mexican food is festive and fun, and we know that a night out at El Bandito is not the time to try and be good and order grilled fish or something stupid like that. That is what LSE* girls do when they are playing small*. Plus if you do this, you'll just end up whiny and jealous of your friends who ordered more fun stuff than you, and start swiping from their giant pile of nachos. That's not hot.

We really don't know what to tell you here, though, because the yummy Mexican food is all pretty much fucked up*. You're just gonna have to go for it. At least try to strategize ahead of time and eat a pound of spinach for lunch when you have plans to go out for Mexican that night.

Here are a few quick tips, though, that will keep you feeling at least light enough on your toes to dance the night away after a few of those aforementioned margaritas: First off, always swap out flour tortillas for corn, which have less than half the calories! Use this trick when you're making quesadillas at home, too. Using corn tortillas makes you feel like you're being all authentic, too.

Also, please don't order nachos as an appetizer - it's kind of ridiculous. They always give you chips and salsa for free, and the last thing you need before a giant Mexican meal of tortilla, meat and cheese is a huge mound of nachos, which are just fried tortillas with meat and cheese!!

One more thing we're going to beg of you is to please stop putting sour cream on things. Come on, you've got so much cheese on there already, right? You will never even taste a spoonful of sour cream, and that very spoonful contains over 100 calories. It's totally not worth it.

One additional quick reminder - we are talking about Mexican food, girls, on which it is totally okay to splurge on once in a while. What we are not referring to in these pages is fast food. You already know how we feel about that. In this case, fast food includes any "Mexican restaurant" that serves powdered guacamole and/or is a chain - and that definitely means Taco Bell. We beseech you to start thinking outside the bell as well as the bun for your own good, ladies, even if Taco Bell already has your heart.

Bambina Italia!

We know that Everybody Want to be Italian,* or at the very least, everybody wants to *eat* Italian! Italian food is delicioso, romantic and comforting, but unfortunately, with all the low-carb, no-carb bullshit that's been going on lately, Italian food has gotten a bad rap. Okay, true, you cannot eat a pound of spaghetti Bolognese every night, unless you are Tony Soprano or want to look like him, but when you do go out for Italian food, you should absolutely enjoy every warm, rich, flavorful bite!

Italian restaurants are places to relax, enjoy and splurge a little bit. That does not mean that you should order bruschetta, calamari, chicken parmesan, a side dish of fettuccini alfredo, a bottle of wine, spumoni AND tiramisu! But you should order what you want. Just like at a Mexican restaurant, if you play small* and order broiled fish with a side of steamed broccoli at an Italian restaurant, we know you are going to fuck up and order Pizza Hut the minute you get home! And you'll also piss of that hot Italian waiter. Italian men love women who love to eat because Italians love to eat, and they love to feed people.

So don't worry about carbs and fat and just enjoy a bit of Italian culture for a night. Sip on a glass of wine, have a slice of that warm freshly baked bread, order a light salad or share a yummy cheesy appetizer, and then order what you want for dinner.

You don't have to eat your entire entree; in fact you probably *shouldn't* end up licking your plate if it was covered with a GIANT piece of meaty cheesy lasagna or pasta smothered in a bucket of cream sauce. We order things like Eggplant Parmesan or Chicken Picatta or seafood pasta in a yummy, light marinara sauce. Then we cover the whole thing with a fuckload of parmesan cheese. It's just as tasty and a lot hotter than your man's jumbo ravioli stuffed with 14 cheeses and covered in three different kinds of meat sauce.

Also, Bella bambina's, we should remind you that you are Hot Chicks, and Hot Chicks do not participate in things like the "never-ending pasta bowls" or "unlimited breadsticks." Enjoy your meal, but it is not your last supper so don't act like it!

American Woman

We know that some of you love the food and drinks at those chain mall restaurants (Applebee's, TGI Friday's, Ruby Tuesday's, Chili's, etc...), and others of you only eat there when you're driving across the country and can't even find a goddam Cracker Barrel. Either way, we have some things for you to think about.

First of all, if you're meeting your friends for drinks because it's TGI Friday time, make sure to follow all of our regular party rules. The mixed drinks at these places can be even sweeter and more deadly than the ones at most bars, so be especially careful of their overpriced, overfattening signature cocktails.

Now, you'll obviously need something to eat along with your cocktails, but we're going to beg you not to order any of those ridiculous looking appetizers that they always show in their commercials! Every single one of them is fried, greasy and way more fattening than your co-worker's birthday cake that you proudly turned down at 3 p.m.

TGIF's even has fried mac 'n cheese on the menu now!! Let's see, what's the one thing you can do to mac 'n cheese to make it even more fucked up*? Oh, yeah - fry it! The last thing you need is to ingest some of this crap before a night of drinking. So if you're just snacking, you should probably take it easy and just get some bread or chips and salsa or something. There is literally nothing else acceptable on these appetizer menus!

If you're going for dinner and not just for drinks, you have a few options to play with, but not many. All of the sandwiches are grilled in partially hydrogenated bullshit so skip those, and most of the salads have chunks of fried chicken on top just to fuck with you! We know you want to order a piece of grilled salmon just to be healthy, and so do we! But don't do it unless you are actually close to a natural body of water. (We made the mistake of ordering salmon at a Chili's in the middle of the desert once and lost more weight than we wanted after throwing it up for days.)

It also sounds like a good idea to hit the salad bar, right? Wrong again. We drove across the country once with our dad and ate from a Ruby Tuesday's salad bar in Ohio. Nothing against Ohio, but that shit was fucked up*. Our trip was soon sidelined for a full 48 hours because we puked all over the steering wheel and had to get our car reapulstered before we could continue.

Anyway, there are some decent and fun things on these menus - try the chicken fajitas, which shouldn't be too bad as long as you instantly throw that giant cup of sour cream they give you over your shoulder (maybe you'll hit a cute guy with it). Or get anything that comes in a skillet - that stuff usually isn't that fucked up* and there's always the added drama of possibly burning yourself at any moment.

The bottom line is, as patriotic as we Hot Chicks are, we have to admit that these places, which proliferate nearly every American town, just aren't that healthy. And when you start eating more and more like a Hot Chick, the blooming onion and sizzling triple meat fundido won't sound so appetizing to you anymore, either.

Maybe you can start convincing your friends to meet up somewhere else, or you can invite them over and serve them some your own hot little appetizers and cocktails! But if you have to go to one of these places, just do you best. Eat half (or less) of your meal and then give your doggie bag to the homeless guy you'd normally try to avoid on the way to your car. Trust us; he needs those empty calories more than you do.

Chinese If You Please

Eating Chinese food is quite popular here in America. Many of us order it in or go out for some good old Dim Sum and have fun with chopsticks at least once a month. And we think it must be healthy since there aren't nearly as many obese Chinese people as there are American. However, we think that those hot little petite gals from China must be blessed with some super duper metabolisms or something.

The other day we wanted some Chinese for dinner, so we went to PF Chang's online to check out the menu. Now, PF Chang's claims to be "healthy Chinese," but when we clicked on the nutrition facts of some of the most popular dishes, we were shocked and heartbroken to realize that almost everything on the menu has like 9 million calories. This totally pissed us off.

How can we enjoy Chinese food without feeling like a sumo wrestler 20 minutes after we finish our Mu Gu Gi Pan? Well, don't worry! We have ways for you to think outside that cute little take-out box so that you'll end up feeling hotter than a steaming egg roll when you open up that little fortune cookie.

Fortune Fact 1 - No Fried Sides

An easy way to cut down on the caloric content of your Chinese dinner is to stay far away from greasy side dishes like fried rice. Fried rice is not just fried rice. It's fried rice with lots of eggs, lots of oils and lots of animal fats. If you are going to eat something fried, we think it's hotter to order some other yummy main dish and keep your side dish light and healthy. Ask for brown rice or just get a small side of that sticky white rice that Asians make so well, and put a little soy sauce on it. Oh, and if it's available, always reach for the low sodium soy sauce. Your brain won't know the difference, but your body will.

Fortune Fact 2 - Chow MAIN, Low MAIN

We think chow mein and low mein noodles are called "mein" for a damn good reason. We don't speak Chinese, be we think the Hot Chick definition of "mein" means it should be your "main" course. Would you go to an Italian restaurant and order creamy seafood linguini AND veal parmesan? Well, we certainly hope not. So why would you eat a plate of greasy noodles as a side dish and also eat a plateful of pork and rice and egg rolls? Did you spend all day chopping wood in 10 feet of snow? We don't think you did, and we sure don't think your body needs all that food.

Fortune Fact 3 - Steam Or Stir It Up

Unless you are at Panda Express (which you shouldn't be, because it is the Chinese equivalent of Taco Bell) there are some dishes on every Chinese menu that aren't fried. Most stir fried dishes have at least 200 calories less than deep fried ones, and steamed versions are about 500 calories less.

Read through that menu or ask your cute kimono-wearing waitress for one of these lighter dishes. Put on a little soy sauce, and you'll feel way hotter than if you ate a bunch of deep fried chicken nuggets dipped in that fake, florescent, corn syrupy orange sauce.

10 Things That Are More Fucked Up Than You Think*

#1 - Maple Syrup

Yes, it comes from a tree and is all natural and does have some good nutrients, but we bet you didn't know that two tiny tablespoons have over 100 calories! And admit it, when you delicately pour this nectar onto your pancakes at brunch, your dainty little wrist is actually flooding your plate with at least half a dozen of those tablespoons. That adds up to about 500 calories just in syrup! Aunt Jamima - what a bitch. We advise that you only use the real stuff - not because it's any lower in calories, but because it tastes more intense and tree-like, and so you'll probably end up using less of it. Pour one or two tablespoonfuls onto the side of your plate, stare in horror at how small a portion that actually is, and learn how to dip.

#2 - Chex Mix

This stuff is delicious. But think about it - why, under normal circumstances, would a handful of cereal, a few pretzels and a bunch of crusty old bread chunks be so tasty? We'll tell you why - because it's coated with a stick of butter and a giant heap of salt. A tiny handful has about 150 calories and half of those are from fat. Gross. If you really want to eat a stick of butter, make like Carrie and go get a delicious cupcake or something, but don't eat it on your cereal.

#3 - Eggplant

We know that many of you think you're being smart when you order an eggplant parmesan sub at your local pizza place. It's a vegetable, so it's gotta be good for you, right? Not so fast, girls. Once it's breaded, fried and slathered with cheese, eggplant ceases to be a vegetable at all - it is a now a giant sponge whose sole mission is to soak up as much grease, oil and lard as possible and deliver it directly into your cute little bod.

#4 - Honey

Like maple syrup, honey is all natural, and many health-conscious ladies pour buckets of it into their tea on a daily basis (except for you super-vegans who feel bad about stealing from the poor little bumble bees). Well, we don't give a shit about bees, but we do care about you, and we want you to know that honey has about 64 calories per tablespoon! A few squirts out of that giant plastic bear and your herbal tea is now equal in calories to a can of Coke. Not what you had in mind, is it?

#5 - Ketchup

Okay, ketchup isn't that bad for you. It's only got about 15-25 calories per tablespoon, which is relatively low. However, you should know that the commercial brands contain mostly sugar, or else it would taste like that terrible tomato paste, wouldn't it? Just be careful about how much of this stuff you use. A few blobs on a veggie burger is fine, but a whole cup of it with a plate of french fries is just gonna add to your problems.

#6 - Tortillas

See our Mexican Restaurant section for more on this, but for now suffice it to say that a giant flour tortilla can add upwards of 200 calories to your burrito or even that healthy wrap. That wouldn't be such a big problem if these things had even the tiniest bit of taste! But tortillas are as bland as can be - you might as well try sucking down two cups of flour for a similar effect. Our solution is to perform a simple surgery on any food that comes to us wrapped. We eat the innards first and then eat the tortilla last and only if we're still hungry. And when we see that giant unrolled thing on our plate, we're usually not.

#7 - Mayo

You probably know that this stuff is bad for you, but you most likely don't know exactly how bad it is! Mayonnaise actually has 90 calories per tablespoon!! That is equal to eating another entire apple for every knife-full that you spread on...whatever you spread it on. Plus, mayo is just gross egg-yolky nonsense, so you should probably stay away from it even in small quantities.

#8 - Rice Cakes

Wait a minute! Rice cakes are diet food, aren't they? Well, yes, but they're also a giant waste of your time. They have about 50 calories each, but they do not fill you up at all, unless of course you eat the whole bag. But if you're gonna go and eat the whole bag, you might as well eat some real food, right?! And please don't try to convince us that you actually like rice cakes, because we simply won't believe you.

#9 - Bubble Teas

This trend seems to be fading, thank goodness, but we still have to mention it. First of all, it is not hot to suck down slimy, gelatinous tapioca balls in your beverage! But putting that aside, these drinks are even worse for you than those frapped coffee concoctions. They usually have between 325 and 450 calories each, which is like adding another meal to your day. We say, save the $5 they ridiculously charge you for these things and eat some gummy bears or even pudding for dessert if you're into this jelly crap.

#10 - Canned Frosting

We don't mean to insult your intelligence; we know that you already know that this stuff is sinful. But you don't know how bad it is. It's got about 75 calories per tablespoon, and when you make cupcakes at home (or eat this junk right out of the can) we know that you're probably using a lot more than that. Frosting is actually one of our favorite things on the planet, but we think that when you're gonna indulge, you should skip this processed, trans-fat-filled bullshit and make frosting from scratch. It's really easy to make, and the real stuff is so intensely delicious that you won't be tempted to eat a whole canful of it. (And if you are, make those cupcakes and bring them into work the next day. You'll be hot and extremely popular instantly.)

Since we're so nice, here's an easy frosting recipe! We recommend adding different food coloring to make your frosting look as pretty as the prettiest bakery's!

Cream 1/3 cup butter, $\frac{1}{4}$ teaspoon salt, and 1 teaspoon vanilla, beating until light and fluffy. Add 3 $\frac{1}{2}$ cups confectioners sugar gradually, beating after each addition. Add 3 tablespoons milk, beating until smooth.

Chapter 8
How to Eat Like a Hot Chick
On a Date

So many girls dread dinner dates, but we don't understand this! If a guy is cute and you like him and he's buying you dinner, you should be so twitterpated* and psyched that you shouldn't know what to do with yourself! Actually, you should. We know that you get nervous about eating in front of you crush - you're thinking about food in your teeth and sauce in your lap or crumbs in your cleavage. But guess what? If you start spending more time with this boy, you're gonna be eating in front of him all the time, too, so you'd better get used to it!

If you follow our rules on what to eat on a date, you will arrive home clean, well-fed and confident enough to bring your date inside with you. And if you fuck up* once in a while and he finds some croutons or something later when he takes off your bra, it's really fine. Boys like snacks at all times, especially after sex, so it's all good.

Dinner Dates

Now, if you're eating out at a restaurant, which is where most dates take place, you should follow all of our regular restaurant rules. But this is also a good opportunity to eat a full, delicious meal and not feel even the tiniest shred of guilt about it. And no, we're not going to tell you to starve yourself all week in order to look hot in your magic* jeans and then pig out on your date so that you look like a carefree vixen with a magic* metabolism. Don't be LSE* -- you are hot. The fact that this boy asked you out in the first place is proof of this, so you don't have to pretend to be anything that you're not.

Despite the way they act sometimes, boys are not dumb. If you play small* and eat a tiny Mary Kate* meal in order to look dainty and restrained, he will know that you're planning on eating a box of Oreos as soon as you get home. We took a poll and a guy friend of ours even said that the hottest thing a girl could do on a date is to eat the way she normally does, so go for it. If it is meant to be, he will even find the quirky way you dismantle your meal or separate your colors adorable, so always be yourself, ladies.

What's really important on a date is *how* you eat, not *what* you eat. We're going to assume that you are totally into this guy you're out with (or we'd have to kick your cute little butt for wasting your time on someone who's not worthy of you), and so you want to be as hot and sexy as possible. The easiest way to do this is to think of your food the same way you would think about having sex with this fella.

(Note: The same is true for them. This is also why we only date guys who love sex and food and aren't even a tiny bit BMS.)*

Unconsciously, guys will assume that your attitude towards whatever's on your plate is exactly the same as your feelings about his body - especially if he bought the food for you. So be selective, but do your best not to come across as *too* picky about every single morsel that you put in your mouth. And whatever you do, don't reject the food altogether, or he may just stop offering you things. Savor every bite, show your appreciation and think about how sexy you look enjoying your food. We promise that he will do everything in his power to get that look of pleasure back on your face later that night.

Sexy Snacks

Some foods, though, are just plain sexy, and it's totally easy to look unbelievably hot while eating them. We asked around and observed many women, and here for you now are the hottest foods you can find. Eat away, bitches.

Sexy Snack #1 - Fruit

Many fruits are naturally sexy, which kind of sucks for us because it's not very often that we get the chance to eat fruit on a date. But if you're on a picnic or whatever, grab a strawberry or two and take a nibble. He'll imagine doing the very same thing to every single part of you. The same thing goes for cherries (which would be hot even without the obvious, crass connotation) and apples. When you bite into a juicy, delicious round little apple, you will remind him of every succulent curve on your body, and this is always a good idea.

Sexy Snack #2 - Meat

Men also think that it's hot when we eat meat, but be warned that there are several caveats here. Steak is definitely hot, because it's hearty and rare and, once again, juicy. (Juicy = Sexy. That's why we girls pay $200 for sweatpants that say it on our ass.) Bacon, sausage, or any other sort of cured meat products, however, are not particularly hot. You can go ahead and eat those at brunch once in a while after you two are already an item, but we'd avoid snacking on Slim Jims for at least the first few dates if we were you.

Sexy Snack #3 - Ice Cream

Ice cream itself isn't that hot. By itself in a dish it's kind of boring and doesn't really turn anyone on. Try eating an ice cream *cone* in front of your cutie, however, and it will be a whole other story. Most likely, there will instantly be so much sexual tension in the room that it will be very difficult for you to continue. We have been there, and it's downright embarrassing. Do it, though. Finish the cone and he will be yours. We promise.

Sexy Snack #4 - French Fries

We know that this might sound counter-intuitive. French fries and fattening and greasy and you may not think that they're particularly hot, but you're wrong! First of all, you really shouldn't be questioning us since we're giving you permission to order French fries in a diet book. But more importantly, your little fingers will look so cute dipping the fries in ketchup and then putting them into your pretty mouth. Your date (or boyfriend) is sure to let his imagination run from there.

Sexy Snack #5 - Lollipops

We were afraid that this might be too obvious, but several of our guy friends downright begged us to put it in here anyway. So in case you didn't already know, pretty much every guy on the planet thinks it's incredibly hot when you lick and/or suck on a lollipop - just don't bite. There. Done and done.

Date Disasters

Now, we know that we said to eat whatever you want on a date and that he'll find your quirks adorable, but there are some foods that might just give a bad impression. *We* know that you're irresistible, but give him a chance to figure that out for himself before you start munching on some really fucked up* shit. Here are some foods that Hot Chicks should avoid, at least on the first few dates. If he's not worth even these tiny sacrifices, dump him immediately and find someone who is.

Date Disaster #1 - Fried Chicken

We already said that chicken makes us itchy, but that's only one reason that we avoid the Colonel (or anything he would cook) on a date. It's just not hot to eat anything that comes out of a bucket or requires the use of a wetnap, and this stuff does both. Fried Chicken also has a terrible reputation for making you gassy as all hell, and while a Hot Chick would never admit to having experienced any type of gas, we will go on record as believing this rumor to be true.

Date Disaster #2 - Creamed Spinach

We will admit that this stuff tastes really good, but let's be clear about one thing - when we talk about eating a pound of spinach, we most certainly are not referring to a pound of the creamed variety. It's a scientific fact that you will gain 3 pounds from eating just one pound of creamed spinach, just because the universe* will be so pissed off at you for eating such a fucked up* version of a healthy food! Plus, if you eat this on a date, those little green chunks are sure to remain stuck in your teeth for days, so forget it.

Date Disaster #3 - Oysters

If you eat oysters on a date, you will look like you're trying too hard to be sexy. Remember, you are hot - you don't need any bullshit aphrodisiacs to turn your date on. Hot Chicks have many other tools for that.

Date Disaster #4 - Spaghetti

It's actually okay to eat spaghetti on a date, but don't you dare make any corny Lady and the Tramp references. Guys actually aren't that into Disney movies, and if your date is, you might be in for an even bigger disaster later.

Date Disaster #5 - Corn On The Cob

We mean, come on, this is pretty obvious. Corn. Teeth. Bad. Steer away at all costs, for real. If you're at a picnic and you're looking for something to eat, go for a fuckload of fruit. There are all of the aforementioned reasons, plus it's way easier to digest and will keep you glowing late into the night. And you thought you needed him for that!

When There's A Man In The House

Many of you pretty girls are rocking the singles' scene, and we're all for that. Have fun! But some of you are in relationships or married and have to deal with keeping food around the house for your guy to snack on and somehow manage not to inhale all of it yourself before you get it home from the grocery store. It's just a sad truth that many (most) guys like to eat fucked up* stuff. And they can get away with it. Some of it is biological and some of it's societal, but the boys we know generally have no issue buying (and eating) giant bags of chips and gallons of ice-cream and boxes and boxes of Hot Pockets and hot dogs and hot wings.

We have to admit that we love this about our guys, but we don't feel very hot when we eat this stuff along with them. But it's hard to buckle down and make yourself a salad when your boyfriend is eating a block of brie on a loaf of bread and washing it all down with a giant bowl of Sugar Crisp cereal!

Well, we have to admit that we eat a little bit more diligently when we are single, and also have more time to spend at the gym when we're not rushing home to sweat some more with our honey. But having a boyfriend is no excuse to eat like him. If you follow our rules for living with your cutie, you will be able to eat with him every night and stay as fine as the day you met.

Live-In Law #1 - Take Initiative

We already said that we know many ways to a man's heart other than his stomach, but we also know that no man in his right mind is gonna turn down a home cooked meal. So the next time your man suggests ordering in meatball subs and you think you're starting to see a giant resemblance to the sub yourself, tell him that you'll be cooking for him tonight instead and make something healthy!

Check out our dinner tips for suggestions, make his portion bigger than yours so that he gets full, and if he balks just remind him how lucky he is that you're cooking for him at all. And remember, you don't have to tell him that it's healthy! Most guys are so clueless about this stuff that he'll think your broiled salmon is truly decadent if you tell him that it is. Don't you just love that about men?

Live-In Law #2 - Play Mouse

So what do you do when your boyfriend buys a bag of Cheeto's, a box of Oreos, a gallon of Breyer's and six boxes of Mac 'n Cheese and then leaves you at home to go shoot hoops with his boys and all you want to do is rip open every single item? You've been eating spinach all week and now you're just dying to finish off a sleeve of Oreos and half a bag of Cheeto's while your *first* box of Mac 'n Cheese cooks. Well, we have a solution that will satisfy you and your waistline - go ahead and open everything and eat a teeny, tiny bit of all of it.

Seriously, you're only really craving a taste of each of these foods, so go ahead and taste them. Eat five Cheeto's and one Oreo. Or even eat just ½ of an Oreo and throw the other ½ out or give it to your dog. Then go ahead and make a box of Mac 'n Cheese and eat like three spoonfuls and that'll be enough of that shit. Give the rest to your starving man when he comes home, or if you don't think you have enough willpower to not eat it all before then, just throw it out! And don't even feel guilty about wasting that crap. He bought those 6 boxes for like a dollar, so who cares? Then eat a spoonful or two of ice cream for dessert, and be done with it.

See? You got to eat everything without eating *everything*. Your boyfriend may start planting mousetraps around the house, thinking that a rodent got to his food, but so what? That'll keep him busy at home while you're at butt class* making yourself even finer.

Live-In Law #3 - On The Side

Some guys just don't think they'll ever feel satisfied unless they eat a giant piece of meat, some sort of starchy bullshit like bread or mashed potatoes and a vegetable or two as well. We love those beefy American men who eat like this, but this is just too much food for us Hot Chicks to handle every night. (Once in a while is fine, girls, but not every night.) So when we want to sit down to dine with our guy but don't want to get too beefy ourselves, we eat the same stuff as him, but we skip the main dish.

We know this may sound crazy, but think about it - if a giant salad can make a meal for you, then a couple of side dishes can, too. Instead of eating his tiny dinner salad or three string beans on the side, eat a giant heap of veggies or a pound of spinach and go ahead and eat the potatoes and bread, too. Then let him supplement this meal with hot dogs and potted meat and you save those calories for chocolate cake when you're famished later after sex.

Live-In Law #4 - When You're Apart

If you don't want to follow these rules and would rather eat manly bullshit with your guy every night, there is something you can do to offset the effects - just be super, extra diligent when he's not around! Eat salads and apples all day long and then indulge in "guy food" when you eat dinner together. Just don't go too far and starve yourself all day to make up for it, or you'll end up eating his weight in veal parmesan ever night, which might freak him out a little bit.

Live-In Law #5 - Share Alike

Having to share your guy's fatty foods may scare the bejeezus out of you, but there is an upside to having a guy around - you can pawn your bullshit food off on him, too! If you're dying to make chocolate chip cookies but know that you'll eat them all in one night if left to your own devices, make HIM cookies! You can eat one or two and nibble at the batter, but you won't be as tempted to finish them all off if he's sitting on the couch looking forward to some warm, gooey deliciousness (in the form of cookies).

You can treat him like your pet in other ways, too, by letting him clear your plate for you, or even giving him the rest of an hors d'oeuvre that you bit into before realizing that it was full of cheesy nonsense. He'll think that you're being all cute and romantic when you shove that ½ of a stuffed mushroom in his mouth, and you're really just saving yourself 20 minutes on the Stairmaster!

Chapter 9
How to Eat Like a Hot Chick During Tough Times

Life is hard, ladies. We know. And the harder life gets, the more we want to curl up on the couch in our sweatpants and our Uggs and nurse a few pints of Ben & Jerry's. Although we fully support indulging in a good, old-fashioned pity party once in a while, we also know that you'll get bored of that after just a few days and want to face the world again in your magic* jeans and stilettos.

But coming out from hibernation will only be harder if your magic* seems are bursting and your feet are overflowing out of your sexy shoes from all of that ice cream. Well, we have had our own ups and downs, and we have found ways to pamper our inner cry babies without sacrificing our outer Hot Chick! Here are our tips for eating well when life ain't so swell.

When You're PMS-ing

Even the hottest of Hot Chicks can get a little crazy during that time of the month. And just to be clear, PMS is a *real* condition, just like LSE.* (*Note: PMS stands for pre menstrual syndrome. "Pre" meaning "before you menstruate," so the next time some jerky guy says, "God, you're such a bitch, you must be on your period," you can tell him, "No, you stupid douche, I don't start for another 5 days!"*) Anyway, some women claim that they don't experience PMS. We think those girls are either lying or else they're not completely human. Maybe they're angels, or maybe they are somehow more evolved than the rest of us. We really don't know, but we will admit that *we* turn into bitchy emotional disasters who want to eat chocolate covered meatball pizza when *we're* PMS-ing.

Before "Aunt Flow comes to town," many of us get 100 times more bloated, grouchy, depressed, and really freaking hungry! We're super irritated and want to kill someone AND we're craving a super-sized meal from McDonalds, but we don't have the willpower to say no to Ronald McDonald, because all our energy is being used to stop ourselves from murdering our gross annoying neighbor. So we eat the double-double, the giant box of fries, and wash it down with an extra large chocolate shake, and then what happens? Yep. We feel even worse! Now we want to burn our stack of bills, shave our head, throw our computer in our boss's face and then crawl in a dark hole and cry until we finally die of dehydration.

So, what's a girl to do every 20-24 days? Well, honestly, we're not totally sure. We haven't really mastered this yet, but we have come up with a few PMS rules to keep us from gaining 25 pounds in 4 days and strangling our man in his sleep. We think that's a pretty big accomplishment.

PMS Do #1 - Follow The Basic Hot Chick Rule

You should know this by now, but we'll say it again. If you end up eating a whole chocolate cake for breakfast, eat a pound of spinach for dinner. Or, if you ordered pizza and fried chicken at 2 a.m., then eat a salad for breakfast the next day.

PMS Do #2 - Exercise!

Exercising increases our endorphins, and that naturally makes us happier. Go to the gym, go for a long walk, or do 3 workout tapes. Whatever your thing is, do it! It'll help with your mood and help burn off all of that chocolate and cheese. Plus, you could use some time to yourself, since no one else wants to be around your bitchy ass right now.

PMS Do #3 - Listen To Your Body

If you're craving meaty fried tacos, it may just mean that you need a little extra iron and fat in you diet. So go to the store, buy a small steak, cook it on your Foreman grill and enjoy every delicious bite of it. You'll satisfy your fatty-meat craving in a healthier way. And then, if you're dying for a roll of cookie dough after your steak, we don't really know what to tell you.

We know from experience that if you eat it you'll be really pissed off and if you don't eat it you'll be really pissed off. Once when we were PMS-ing, we broke down and cried because we wanted chocolate cake and didn't get to our favorite bakery until after it closed, so maybe you should ask someone else for advice about this.

PMS Do #4 - Make Plans

When we're totally PMS-ing, it's very easy to isolate ourselves. We know how it is, and it's getting worse as we get older - yikes! Sometimes when you feel fat and gross and sad and angry and ugly, the only thing that sounds fun is to eat a box of chocolates inside your duvet cover. Well, girls, that is only going to make things worse.

Stop hating yourself and get out of the house. Make plans with your friends for a nice healthy dinner somewhere fun. Or if you're dying for a gallon of cookies and cream, take your man out for an ice cream cone. Or take a walk in the sunshine and get one of those iced blended coffee things, or grab a slice of pizza and enjoy it in public. We don't really care what you do, just do something that will keep you from eating your whole house all alone inside of it. Pop some Advil, get dressed up, head out into the big beautiful world and eat like a Hot Chick. You'll feel way better.

PMS Do #5 - Do It!

Yep. We mean sex. And this really has nothing to do with

food, unless you're into that kind of thing. But when you're in the heat of the moment, the last thing that should be on your mind is a BLT drizzled in caramel. Sex is a mood booster, just like any other exercise, and it can actually help relax all those girly parts and pieces that are knotted up and crampy.

Now, we're not condoning any unprotected one night stands, and if you're under 18, you really shouldn't be having sex at all yet. But for those of us in relationships, sex can be a great way to combat PMS. Plus, aren't your boobs bigger? And aren't you usually more heydayish* when you're PMS-ing anyway? The only problem is, if you're too bitchy and self-hating, your man may want to stay away from you for a few days. If that's the case, just tackle him or do it by yourself.

When You're Broke

Just because you have $12 in your bank account, that doesn't mean that you should be eating Big Macs all day or slurping down Mac 'n Cheese until your next paycheck. (Why is there always a Mac involved with shitty food?) Instead, this is an excuse to shave off a few extra calories that you can't afford, and pretty soon you'll feel great about how little you can subsist on. Okay, maybe that's a little Mary Kate* of us, but whatever. We're trying to save you money.

Pizza is always good when you're broke, and you won't feel guilty about it if you can only afford one slice. If you're craving frozen yogurt but don't want to waste the money on a snack, get some at midday and call it lunch.

Pasta and bottled sauce is cheap, of course, but we have a better (and even cheaper) alternative when you're craving something creamy and cheesy like polenta or fettuccine alfredo - make some oatmeal and mix in a little bit of salt and a fuckload of parmesan cheese! We know this sounds crazy, but it's actually super-delicious. Plus, a tub of oats can feed you for weeks on only around $3.

Another great way to eat cheap is to fill yourself with free samples at your local overpriced grocery store! Grab a basket and circulate for a while, retrying the same salsa, cheese cubes and one ounce cups of smoothie until you're full. Not only will you get a free lunch, but this is also a great way to eat tiny bits of fattening foods without having to worry about self control. The store manager will probably throw you out before you're able to consume too many calories, anyway.

The point is, there's nothing wrong with eating something small that your mom wouldn't necessarily call dinner. Not only will you save money, but you'll look hotter and be even more appreciative the next time a cutie wants to take you out for a giant meal.

Holiday Help

Holidays can be another tough time to eat like a Hot Chick. Almost every month there seems to be some sort of reason to celebrate, and unless it's Yom Kippur, food is always included in those holiday festivities. January starts off with New Year's parties, which are filled with tons of alcohol and hundreds of fattening finger foods. February is Valentine's Day, which is either a time to lick chocolate off your loved one's nipples or eat a giant box of chocolates alone as you drip tears all over your own.

In March and April there's either Easter or Passover (for most of us), which gives us yet another excuse to scarf chocolate bunny heads or eat pounds of fried potato latkes. In May we have Cinco de Mayo, which forces us to eat hundreds of chips smothered in salsa and guacamole and wash it down with 5 salty margaritas. And don't forget about Memorial Day BBQ's. That's another good opportunity to fatten ourselves up right before bikini season.

June is always someone's birthday, and we love those Gemini's so we've got to help them eat their birthday cake. July starts off with fireworks and usually a keg of beer and heaps of potato salad. In August and September there are always more birthdays, and our favorite men are Virgos, so that's trouble. October has the horror of Halloween candy on every corner, and November starts the big holiday season with Thanksgiving, when we all decide to stuff ourselves even more than the bird on our table.

And December is just ridiculous - except for you poor, lonely Jews on Christmas. But you guys are probably once again drowning your sorrows in potato latkes (which are just glorified hash browns for all of you non-chosen people).

So now that we've scared ourselves by putting in print all the potential times to fuck up* in a year, we're gonna give you a few little hints on how to help you feel hot during all these precarious holidays.

Holiday Hint 1 - Eat, Drink, And Be Merry

Yep, that's right. The number one rule for a Hot Chick is to have fun. So we want you to go out, take your hair down, kick your four inch heals up and celebrate, dammit! Don't for a second think that you are not allowed to eat a slice of apple pie, or have a plate of BBQ ribs. Enjoy every little bite you take at that holiday party, don't feel guilty about it, and then the next day, eat a pound of spinach and run a couple extra miles on the treadmill.

And what if the next day there is another party? Then maybe steer away from the cheese and crackers and just munch on the veggies and dip. Or fuck it! Just go ahead and splurge (within reason) for one more night. But that is it! Partying too many days in a row is guaranteed to take a toll. Or create a fat roll. And you don't want that to keep you from fitting into that cute little outfit you bought for next month's holiday, right?

Holiday Hint 2 - Remember The Power Of Will-Power

Okay, we just gave you full permission to live it up in hint #1, but here we must remind you to use all that willpower you've got burning in your hot little bodies. Think of a holiday just like any other day. If you wouldn't eat 5 doughnuts at your morning office meeting, then don't eat five cookies at your office Christmas party. (Sorry, "*Holiday* Party.") And you would never eat two sandwiches for lunch, right? So don't think you can have a hotdog *and* a hamburger at that pool party.

A holiday is a time to enjoy yourself, so do that, but you still have to use just a little bit of willpower and not hang out all night at the buffet table. If you think you need to eat 2 of everything to have fun, we promise you're wrong. You won't feel hot, and don't you have more fun when you feel hot?! We want you to stay up late and unzip your magic* jeans to bang your boyfriend in the bathroom, not leave early in a food coma and unzip your jeans because you can't breathe.

Holiday Hint 3 - Look At Your Calendar

We've all done this. Every Hot Chick has said at least once in her life, "I'm just gonna eat whatever I want this holiday, and then I'll go on a hard core diet." It's the *all or nothing* mentality. It is the belief that this is the last time we're gonna have the chance to eat 10 pieces of pizza and 10 cupcakes. Well, we are here to remind you to look at your calendar (or just re-read the first paragraph of this section) and realize that in just two to four weeks you will in fact have another chance to celebrate – another chance to have chocolate cake and fried chicken and baked brie.

And are you really gonna stick to your lame-ass diet when this stuff is around? We don't think you are. So you don't have to eat *everything* in sight during Christmas! In just 5 days you'll be celebrating again, and we want you to ring in the new year with some hot guy's hand on your ass, not an extra 5 inches on your ass.

Family Feuds

We love our family, but we don't always love what our family does to us. Going home to visit family can somehow turn us back into a bitchy twelve year old, and sometimes that bitchy twelve year old can't stop opening cupboards or get her pretty little head out of the fridge. Freud and Dr. Phil probably have some cool reason to explain why it is that when we go home to our mothers we want to eat her whole house. We know that it is obviously something emotional.

It's fucking hard to go home sometimes! It's hard to not argue with our stubborn brother or hold in our tears when our dad gets mad at us because we're not married yet or not slit our wrists when our aunt won't talk to us because she thinks we're a giant slut.

We're pretty sure it's all this crazy stress that makes us want to eat *all* the popsicles in the freezer and then the *whole* tray of left-over lasagna. But maybe your family is totally cool? Maybe *you* just want to eat everything because it's *free* or because you haven't had good home cookin' in a while? Whatever the case is, we want you to love and enjoy your family, and then go back to *your* kitchen feeling happy and hot.

Advice for this one is tough because we all have different families, and all our families eat different things. We can't keep you from wanting to stab your step-dad in the face with your fork, but we can help keep you from putting that fork into your mouth way too many times.

Family Fact #1 - Eat 3 Square Meals

Enjoy your family's home cooking by eating breakfast, lunch and dinner. This will: a) keep you feeling satisfied and not deprived, b) keep your Aunt Patsy from worrying that you're pulling a Mary Kate,* and c) it will keep your blood sugar stabilized, which will prevent binges and big stupid petty fights with your little sister.

Family Fact #2 - Lend A Helping Hand

Now that you know how to eat like a Hot Chick, why don't you get your hot ass into the kitchen and help you mamma cook? You can show your family ways to make things healthier but still taste really good! Or if you happen to hate your mamma's cookin,' then quit acting like a child and crying into your plate of tuna casserole and just make something for yourself.

Family Fact #3 - Don't Be Stupid

There really isn't a nicer way to put this. We think you are hot, and we know you are smart, so why do stupid shit that will just make you feel disgusting later? Don't eat the whole loaf of banana bread just because your step mom's ugly poodle ate your favorite shoes! You don't even really like banana bread! And you do not need to eat a box of cheese crackers with a hunk of salami just because your dad is eating it while he watches the game and you're trying to bond.

You also do not need to eat up the entire pantry just because that shit's free. You are not a frat boy; you are a Hot Chick, so treat your body well and ignore your lame cousin that hates you! She's just LSE* and jealous of every hot step you take.

When You've Got Roommate Trouble

Some of you hot young ladies may still live at home with your parental units, but we've already tackled how to eat like a Hot Chick when your mamma makes maple muffins every morning. Now it's time to talk about the living situation that can be even more difficult (in many ways) than living with family and that's living with *roommates!*

Don't get us wrong, roommates can be awesome and super fun. But let's be honest, you may not want to take diet advice from them. We've had every kind of Mary Kate* roommate on the planet - the bulimic chick, the diet pill addict, the girl who hid cans of Campbell's Chunky Beef Soup under her bed (seriously), the girl who ate popcorn ever-so-slowly out of a tiny bowl while counting every single kernel, the chick who only ate pretzels, Jell-O, and gummy bears because they were "fat free," and finally, the "obsessed-with-us roommate," who watched, counted and commented on everything that touched our lips, and yes that included men.

We'd love to give you advice on how to choose good girlfriends and roommates to spare you from having to deal with some of the same psychos that we've lived with, but that's another book. What we will do, though, is give you a few tips on how to eat like a Hot Chick when you're cohabitating with girls who aren't doing so hot themselves.

Roomie Rule #1 – Realize What You're Dealing With

When you are living with roommates and start trying to eat like a Hot Chick, you must first understand that your roomies might totally freak out. If they know that you are trying to lose weight and/or be healthier, they will get all up in your business and ask you 20 million questions. You have to understand that they are just doing this because they are women, and unfortunately most women have insecurities when it comes to food and weight. So when they see *you* trying to better yourself, it reminds them that they may not be treating *their* bodies well.

Or maybe you have a roommate that just naturally looks like a Victoria's Secret model. She may freak out and get jealous that soon you may be "the hot one" instead of her. Don't let this get you down; this is *their* shit, not yours. When your roommate starts acting weird, just remind yourself that it's just her LSE* acting up. Simply acknowledge and dismiss, okay?

Roomie Rule #2 – Organize The Kitchen

This is a *must* when living with roommates, whether you're eating like a Hot Chick or not. In order to keep your slutty roommate's twelve boyfriends from eating all of your healthy, fun food, you're gonna have to go ahead and get a little anal. (Ahem. We mean you should get organized and a bit uptight; leave the other kind to her.) Divide up space in the fridge, write your name on your diet coke, and assign cupboards to all who live in your house. Your roommates will probably still look and see what you've got in your section, but staring at your name will at least make them feel really guilty when they start digging at your peanut butter with their fingers.

Roomie Rule #3 - Only Eat If You Are Hungry

Living with roommates can sometimes be a total diet disaster. It's rare when everyone in your house eats at the same time, and it's really tempting to have a few bites whenever someone else is cooking. And we know how fun it is to go along for the ride to Taco Bell at 3 a.m. But if you have already eaten dinner, you do not need to make another giant pot of macaroni and cheese just so you have an excuse to hang out with your roomie when she comes home.

Even if she offers you a bowl to you to snack on while she tells you all about the professor she's boinking, don't do it. You can sit there and listen and let her know that sleeping with a married man will only come back and bite her in the ass in 5 years when she's so bloated from all that mac 'n cheese that nobody else will want to.

Roomie Rule #4 - Mind Your Own Business

This is where we play by the Golden Rule. If you don't want your roommate watching every morsel you put in your mouth, then you need to leave her alone, too. That means that you do not give her diet advice, you do not tell her that her frozen dinner is bullshit, and you do not roll your eyes when she is blending her protein shake in the morning. Let her eat whatever and whenever she wants.

If she asks for your advice on how to be hot, then, *and only then,* can you help her out. Again, chicks can get weird when it comes to food, so don't make it worse by judging what she eats. It's none of your business and you have enough to worry about, so stop it.

Roomie Rule #5 - Have Your Cake And Eat It Too

We have to repeat the sad, lame truth again - some chicks get really weird about diets, and your roommate might *totally* throw a hissy-fit if she wakes up and sees your hot little ass eating chocolate cake for breakfast. She'll get all fussy and say shit like, "How can you *eat* that? If I ate that for breakfast I'd weigh 500 pounds! It's not fair! Waaaaah!!" Well, what Miss Roomie doesn't understand, (because she foolishly isn't reading this book) is that after you enjoy your cake you will spend an hour on the treadmill and then have a pound of spinach for dinner. Right?

So, our point here is, don't let your roommates make you feel bad about your food choices. Being a Hot Chick means not playing small* and apologizing for who you are. So don't stop eating your cake just because it will prevent her from feeling weird; that's her LSE*, not yours. Just eat your cake, get your ass to the gym, and let her sit and home feeling sorry for herself. Hopefully she'll catch on one of these days, buy this book and work it out.

Uh Oh!! Crunch Time!

This happens to the best of us, ladies. We get carried away having way too much fun eating and drinking, and them BAM! We get hit with an invitation to some very important event where we need to look and more importantly *feel* hot, but instead we feel grosser than road kill.

It could be your boyfriend's best friend from childhood's wedding and three of your man's ex-girlfriends will be there - totally gross, but very important to squash your LSE* and look and feel your best. Or maybe it's a high school reunion or some big important work function and you have one of those ridiculous jobs where you could get fired if you look like shit? Whatever the occasion, we have all at some point felt the pressure to starve ourselves so that we could fit into our little pink dress and impress everyone that lays eyes on us.

Well, we must tell you that starving yourself and spending 18 hours a day at the gym is not going to do the trick. And those silly liquid diets that claim to help you lose 10 pounds in two days are also a bunch of bullshit. They'll just set you up to gain it all back the instant you take your first sip of wine, not to mention what they'll do to your attitude! You will be cranky, irritable and you will hate the whole fucking world! And that defeats the whole purpose of feeling hot. Hot Chicks do not walk around with bitchy, hateful looks on their faces.

So what does a girl do when there is a hotness emergency and she does in fact have to loose 5 pounds in 5 days? Well, we can't get you from a size 12 to a size 2 in 24 hours, but we can offer some little tricks that will at the very least get you to that event with a sassy smile on your face and a sexy skip in your step.

C - Count Calories!

Yes, we told you earlier not to count your calories, but remember, this is an emergency! Only from now until the event, you must count pretty much every single morsel you put into your mouth and write everything down. This will keep you honest and stop you from unconsciously grabbing a handful of chocolate kisses as you leave the dentist's office. Go back and read the calorie section for more on this, but we suggest about 1,400 calories a day when you need to sport that hot little mini skirt in a week.

R - Run!

If your boobs are too big or you have bad knees and can't run, then walk - fast! Or ride a bike - for a really, really long time. Whatever you can get yourself to do, find a way to sweat buckets for at least an hour a day. You might have to wake up a couple of hours earlier or skip your lunch break with your cute co-worker and eat an apple and almonds on the way to the gym, but that's okay. It won't kill you to push yourself for a few days, and think about how much hotter you'll be by lunchtime next week.

U - Use Your Friends!

Feeling stressed and pressured can often make us feel alone, and feeling alone makes us depressed, and feeling depressed makes us want to eat a giant gallon of cookie dough ice cream. So don't isolate yourself. Use your friends! That's what they are there for. Invite them to exercise with you, or suggest that you toss a giant salad together one night instead of going out for sushi and martinis. It'll be good for them, too, to have a week of being healthier, so everybody wins.

N - Never Complain

Just in case you didn't know, it is not hot to complain about feeling fat, needing to loose weight, or that you can't eat a club sandwich because you're on a diet. Seriously ladies, shut up. No one cares. And talking about how gross you feel or how mad you are about having to exercise just makes other people feel LSE.* It makes them look at their own thighs and feel bad about the french fries they ate at lunch. Hot Chicks do not make other chicks feel like shit, so stop complaining about what you need to do and just do it!

C - Cut It Out!

You should already be counting calories and following all of our rules on how to eat like a Hot Chick. However, you are going to have to cut out a few other things in order to feel extra amazing in a short amount of time. Cut out ALL processed food, ALL white flour, ALL sugars, and ALL added fats, and

ALL sodium. This may sound a bit Mary Kate*, but it's really not that hard. It just means that you eat a salad at lunch instead of a sandwich and a banana for a snack instead of frozen yogurt and bulk candy. Or leave the cheese out of your omelet and cook your fish without oil.

All of these little adjustments to your food will save you hundreds of calories, which will absolutely make a difference on the scale and how many heads you turn on your big night. When the event is over, put the cheese and the candy back in, but only the normal amount! You don't have an excuse to pig out just because you restrained yourself for one week, or you'll end up feeling worse than you did before doing all of this work, which is not the point.

H - Hydrate!

We have already given you a million different ways to drink water, so there is just no excuse for not doing it. Drink that water until you feel like you're gonna pop, and don't worry about retaining it. Your body will adjust, and all that extra water will actually help your body remove any water weight that you already had! How cool is that?

T - Talk Nice!

It is very important for Hot Chicks to treat others with respect, but we often forget to treat ourselves with respect. Be nice to yourself, ladies! Don't tell yourself that you're fat or get mad at yourself for not being in shape or waste time feeling guilty about the bowl of cake batter you ate last week. Let it go. You can't change the past, but you *can* change the future, and it all starts with knowing that you can do it. If you say awful things to yourself, you will eventually start believing them, and then you will just make those awful things come true!

The longer you talk shit to that little roll that hangs over your jeans, the longer it will stay there and piss you off. We're not quite sure how this happens – we're pretty sure it has something to do with the universe* believing what we tell it about ourselves. But this can work in our favor, too, ladies! If you start telling yourself and the universe* that you're hot, pretty soon you will indeed be hot, so start thinking positively now.

I - Imagine!

We don't just want you to eat like a Hot Chick; we want you to think like a Hot Chick. And when a Hot Chick wants something, she thinks about it – a lot. Do you want to slide into those skinny jeans on Saturday night, but it's Monday and you can't get the top button closed? Well, imagine yourself putting them on, having them fit, and then feeling like the sexiest girl in the world at your event. Have a little fantasy sequence* about what you are going to look and feel like in 5 days. We know this may sound creepy to some of you, but it's crunch time, right? Don't waste time judging, just try it!

M - Make It Happen!

If a boxer needs to weigh in on Friday, but is four pounds over his weight class limit on Wednesday, what do you think he does? Does he cry to all of his friends about how fat he is or does he get his ass in the gym and watch what he eats?! We think you know the answer. So girls, if you want to lose a few before that big thingy you have, take a little lesson from the boys, and just make it happen.

Make exercising, counting calories, and drinking water a priority. And don't say that you're too busy - that's crap. We are the two busiest gals we know, and we can make time for crunch time, and so can you! If you want it bad enough, we know you can use your hot little head to figure out how to make it happen.

E - Eat!

This book is called How to *Eat* Like a Hot Chick, not How to *Starve* Like a Hot Chick. Yes, even when it is crunch time, you still must eat. Lots of women don't realize this, but dieting isn't about *not* eating, it's about *eating,* and eating often. But you have to eat the right things. And if your options are limited on those days during which you have to shrink considerably, then we suggest you only eat things that come from our hot mother Earth. Go to the grocery store and stock up on tons of fruit and veggies, oats, nuts, and throw in a little lean protein for the evening.

Make sure you eat breakfast, lunch, dinner, and even have a couple of snacks. But again, watch your calories! You can't eat 4 avocados and a jar of peanuts just because they come from the Earth, but we sincerely hope that you know that by now.

Food Props - In Case Of A Hotness Emergency

Okay, so maybe you fucked up* and didn't do any of that stuff and your big event is *tomorrow*, or maybe you just bought this book and didn't have time to implement our advice. Or maybe you felt fine yesterday but just woke up feeling like shit today and have to look extra hot tonight. Is it your ex-boyfriend's birthday party, or are you just feeling extremely heydayish* and planning on hitting the town hard? We know that there are some times when even your best makeup, big hair, spray tan, magic* jeans and booby shirt just won't cut it, and you need to pull out all the stops.

You may not realize it, but in these cases food can be your best friend. Use these tricks to help your food make you look, feel and just *be* the hottest girl in any room, bar none. Now girls, proceed with extreme caution. If you use more than one of these at any given time, you'll probably end the night with a giant case of OWL* syndrome after an all-out rumble breaks out amongst the 37 boys who are vying for your attention. Have fun.

Food Prop #1 - A Candy Necklace

This is especially helpful if you need to look really hot but are for some silly reason temporarily hating everything about your body. We totally understand - that happens to all of us. Remember, no matter how fat or bloated you feel, your neck will always look slender and pretty, and it's ultra-important to draw attention to those parts of your body that you definitely don't have to worry about.

We love to strap on one of those old-school candy necklaces whenever we want every boy in the room to be focused on us from the neck up, or especially on our necks. What better way to make you feel sexy than to have a bunch of guys fighting to bite at and lick your neck? Trust us, you'll feel hot even before the first piece of candy is off of the string.

Food Prop #2 - A Giant Bowl Of Jell-O Shots

This has worked for us at numerous parties, and we're super psyched to pass this tip on! For the next party you host or attend, prepare a bowl of your favorite color Jell-O with the requisite $\frac{1}{2}$ water and $\frac{1}{2}$ vodka (or if you and a group of friends all need to feel hot, make a bowl for each of you). When party time comes, work your way around the crowd with the bowl in hand, and deliver spoonfuls of this magic* formula into the mouths of fellow partygoers. We know this isn't the most hygienic of ideas, but whatever - that's what our immune systems are for.

Now, of course you can pay special attention to the cutest boys at the party and give them the most Jell-O. The very act of spooning this stuff into their mouths is dead sexy. Plus, not only will you be a beautiful little goddess gifting them with mouthfuls of goodness, but they'll get tipsier with each and every mouthful, and soon their "Jell-O goggles" will obscure any imperfections that might be distracting you.

In The Air!

Some of us Hot Chicks do a ton of traveling for our jobs. This may seem glamorous to those of you out there who feel stuck behind a desk, but trust us, it is NOT easy or fun to live out of a suitcase. And it is 100 times harder to feel hot when you are on the road. Airplane food combined with jet-lag can make you feel as gross as if you just shared a bucket of KFC with your lecherous boss on the first day of your period. Anyway, we have a few suggestions to help you feel hot even when you spend 75% of your life in and out of airports on those boring, lonely, exhausting business trips.

A - Always Eat Before You Leave Your House

If you have an early flight, eat breakfast beforehand. If it's in the afternoon, make sure you have breakfast *and* lunch. Whatever you do, do not go to the airport starving. It will just make you want to strangle the mean security man when he tries to confiscate your lip gloss. Plus, there is never anything good to eat at the airport, and you probably won't have time to search for something healthy. You'll only end up asking for 12 bags of peanuts as soon as you board the plane. None of this is good, so do a little pre-emptive strike and eat before you leave.

I - Imitate Your Life At Home

Being in a different time zone does not mean that you can cheat on your boyfriend and not have it count, and it also doesn't mean you can eat shitty food and not have it count! Both have severe consequences that may stick with you for some time. When you're on the road, try as hard as you can to eat whatever you would normally eat for breakfast, lunch and dinner at home. If you would not eat a McDonald's McGriddle for breakfast at home, then you have no excuse to do it when you're traveling.

It may be really hard to find good things to eat in the middle of nowhere or in a crowded airport, but come on! We know you can do better than fast food. Get a cup of coffee and buy an apple and a package of nuts from the little magazine stand near your gate. Or if you can't find that, let this be a rare time when you have a protein bar. It's not the best, but it is closer to what you should be eating.

R - Remember Water

Being at 35,000 feet is extremely dehydrating, ladies! They say you should drink 8 ounces of water for every hour you fly just to fight off the puffiness and jet lag caused by dehydration. Well, we've taken their advice (whoever *they* are) and it totally works. We feel way hotter on flights when we drink a fuckton of water than we do when we pound beer and diet coke. So guzzle that H2O, girls!!

You may be worried about pissing off the guy in the aisle seat when he has to get up every time *you* have to piss, but seriously, he won't mind that much, because you're hot! And having an ass as hot as yours three inches from his face six times in three hours is the best thing that's happened to him in a long time.

P - Pack A Snack

First, make sure it's not liquid, or anything else recently banned by the FAA or TSA. But we are sure that you have room in that cute little carry-on for a healthy mini-meal. Pack fruit, nuts, a sandwich, or whatever your little heart desires. It'll keep you from eating shitty airplane food and save you some money and calories if you've got a layover and are forced to eat that overpriced bullshit at the airport.

L - Let Them Keep It

Some may claim that airplane food has gotten better over the years, but they are totally full of shit. Unless you're flying first class, most of it tastes terrible and is full of terrible things. Are you really going to eat a beef stroganoff or a chicken sandwich that is sealed in plastic and has been in some weird refrigerator at 35,000 feet for a couple of days? Really? Can't you just eat the snack you packed and wait 3 more hours to eat something substantial and tasty when you land? We think you can. We think that when the flight attendant tries to give you a package of processed crap you should just let her keep it.

A - Altitude + Sodium = Puffiness

Yep. If you eat that airplane food or buy that five dollar snack box that is full of Doritos, Cheez Wiz and Chips Ahoy, you will arrive at your destination with an extra 5 pounds of bloat. You'll still be kinda cute, but no one's gonna ask you to join the mile high club anytime soon because that extra 1,000 calories and 100,000 grams of sodium is sure to make your face, fingers and toes all puff up like a Thanksgiving day parade float.

N - Never Get Really Wasted

Again, if you happened to be in first class and they fill up that cute mini wine glass for free, go ahead and knock back a few. But if you're flying in coach and it's costing you 5 dollars for 2 ounces of alcohol, we suggest just having maybe one to calm your nerves. We're not giving you financial advice, we're telling you to watch your alcohol intake so that you won't arrive at your destination with a huge headache and a puffy face.

Because of the dehydration thing that happens when you're stuck in a giant piece of metal that's flying through the air really fast, too much alcohol will make you feel like complete dog shit. Plus, please don't be that annoying drunk girl who might end up puking on that poor guy in the aisle if there's turbulence.

E - Eliminate Your Stress

Traveling is stressful, period. It doesn't matter if you're going to Hawaii on holiday or the armpit of Ohio for business, there is always a good chance that you will become infected with OWL Syndrome* when you travel. There is too much to remember, too many rules, too many lines, too many crowds, too many delays, too many asshole airline attendants and too much shitty food tempting you to "comfort" you during this high stress time!

We can't tell you where you put your passport or help make you less homicidal during your 6 hour layover, but we can offer some advice on how to not make yourself feel even worse. Don't make a shitty, stressful situation even shittier by stuffing your face with shitty food! It'll taste kinda good at the moment, but in 20 minutes you'll be in an even worse mood and feel even more lethargic as you lug your laptop 10 miles to your gate and then sit smashed in between a guy who should have bought 2 seats and another who's manically chewing his fingernails and spitting them on your Sky Mall magazine. Eliminate your stress by not stress eating!

Work It Out

Hot Chicks work out. They just do. They find time for it, they don't question it, and they certainly don't sit around complaining that they really should be doing it. We'll save our real workout tips - from how to do everything from build a brand new ass to make a new best friend at the gym - for our next book, but right now let's talk about how food relates to working out.

We often see girls scarfing down Snickers bars and saying things like, "I worked out this morning, so it's okay for me to eat this." Not quite. First of all, it's never hot to reward yourself with food like you're some sort of cat in a puzzle box. But also, these girls are fucking up their math. If you do a half an hour of cardio, you'll burn about 150 calories, and a regular Snickers bar has 280. You don't even need a calculator to see that this is fucked up*. Even if you go for a full hour of cardio, which is a LOT, you'll only get rid of about 300 calories, and by the time you eat the damn Snickers you're still only down 20. That's right, 20 calories after slaving away for an hour on the Stairmaster!!*

You just can't use food as a reward for working out. And let's be honest - unless you're competing in a triathlon or something crazy like that, you don't actually need extra food to get through your workout. So don't fall for those bars and smoothies and "healthy" muffins that they bombard you with the minute you walk through those gym doors. And don't buy special water to drink while you're working out, either! You really don't need it. Just go to the gym, drink your giant bottle of regular water while you sweat away, and you'll walk out glowing and feeling way hotter than you did when you walked in. We promise.

Chapter 10
Extra Goodies

Hottie At Home

Now that you know how to eat like a Hot Chick, you better get your house all set up to do so. First, you need to clean up your house like a Hot Chick, and we're not talking about dressing up in a slutty French maid costume and bending over to dust and vacuum for your new hubby. That's another book. We mean to clean out the old cupboards. Remove anything that keeps you from eating like a Hot Chick, and that includes everything that calls your name at midnight. (Unless it's your boyfriend making you feel particularly heydayish* at midnight. Don't get rid of him.)

Really, you know that if you have those delicious Dove bars in your freezer, you're gonna eat one (or six) every night. Keep it out of the house and then go get an ice-cream cone after sex with your sweetie! Doesn't that sound way more fun? Anyway, after you have donated your big bags of Costco chips to the boys and girls club and dumped gallons of ice cream down the garbage disposal, it's time to restock your home with tons of good food that you should always have within your toned arms' reach.

Hot Buys

Some of you may already be amazing in the kitchen and be able to shop smart and cook healthy meals. Well, good for you! But we know that there are hundreds of Hot Chicks out there that are totally clueless about what to have in the fridge that is both healthy and totally fun. We know that grocery shopping isn't easy; it can be really tempting to bypass the produce and go home with a frozen dinner and a yummy box of Entenmanns's bullshit.

We decided it would be cool to give you a few ideas of what to fill your fridge with. By now, you should know what the fuck to do with this stuff once you have it in your house. Here's your shopping list.

Almonds -- Have a handful for a snack or have your man try to throw them in your cleavage!
Apples, bananas, peaches, grapes, and any other fruit you like - Snack time for Hot Chicks.
Avocados - Spill them over your dining room table for a beautiful bounty.
Balsamic Vinegar - Splurge on the fancy stuff just once!
Brown rice - It's waaaaay healthier than white rice. And it has fiber! Yay!
Cans of soup - Read the labels carefully! But keep these on hand in case you get sick.
Cans of Tuna fish - Don't pull a Jessica Simpson. Dumb is not hot!!
Eggs - Yum, yum, chicken fetus.

Flavored Seltzer - You can even mix it with Vodka for a fun cocktail hour at home.
Frozen Veggie Burgers - Only to be used in emergencies.
Goat cheese, feta, or another kind of non-processed Cheese - The best aphrodisiac we can think of when paired with a bottle of wine and a cute boy.
I Can't Believe It's Not Butter - Thanks, Fabio! We can't believe it, either.
Lean protein of your choice (chicken, fish, or even cans of beans) - Whatever doesn't make you itchy.
Mustard - Any kind will do. It's that awesome.
Oatmeal - Quick cooking is fine but not the packets.
Pam (Or any other non-stick spray. We're not getting paid by the nice people at Pam or anything) - Grease those pans and skip the oil.
Parmesan Cheese - Try it freshly grated instead of in a big green tub.
Red wine, white wine, light beer, and a bottle of cheap champagne - Essential for evenings in with your man.
Salsa - Tons of flavor and NO calories! How hot is that?
Spices - Buy a giant selection to help spice up your life! Not that you need it.
Spinach - How else could you eat pounds and pounds of it?
Splenda - No cancer for you Hot Chicks!
Tomatoes, mushrooms, peppers, onions, garlic, cucumber, carrots, broccoli, asparagus, radishes, and any other veggie that you'll eat - Raw is best but frozen will do in a pinch. Nothing canned, ladies!
Whole grain bread - Get the super nutty kind!

Live It!

Now that you beautiful ladies have all of the information you need about how to *eat* like a Hot Chick, we want you to just take down your hair and start *living* like a Hot Chick. Don't start obsessing about your food and exercise; just *trust* that you now know exactly how to eat and treat your body well and notice how hot and powerful that knowledge makes you feel. And you know that the hotter you allow yourself to feel, the more invisible all of your imperfections will become, even to you!

We know that we just gave you a whole bunch of diet advice, but HOW TO EAT LIKE A HOT CHICK is not a diet. It is just a bunch of tools to help you realize how beautiful your body is and how easy it can be to enjoy your favorite foods *and* enjoy feeling sexy.

We already told you that we wrote this book because we felt the need to remind you that you are hot. And now we want to give you permission to start acting like you're hot. It's all in your pretty little heads, ladies, so just let yourself be whoever you want to be. Quit complaining, quit pinching your thighs when you get our of the shower, quit telling yourself that you'll stop eating carbs on Monday, and stop comparing yourself to botoxed, lipo-sucked, saline enhanced, fake tanned, airbrushed celebrities who pay people to help them look hot.

When you stop expending all that energy on useless negative bullshit and use it instead to do positive things for yourself and think positive thoughts, you will be amazed at the results.

So tonight, we want you to break open a cheap bottle of champagne, eat your favorite food for dinner, and celebrate the fact that you are hot. Say goodbye to all those days you've wasted feeling like shit or telling yourself that you look like shit, and get ready for your fun, hot new life. We know that it's a bit scary, because all change is, but we also know that you can handle it. We can't wait to hear about the results. Have fun!

xo,

Jodi & Cerina

Glossary, Hot Lingo or How to Talk Like a Hot Chick

BMS: This stands for Bill Merrit Syndrome. Bill Merrit is one totally gross guy we dated, but he shares an affliction with many men who also suffer from *BMS*. The primary symptom is when a man uses his busy, important work schedule as an excuse to shut out the possibility of love or a relationship, or even some fun crazy messy sex. Secondary symptoms include being totally LSE* about sex and being stingy with compliments. Men with this syndrome tend to keep their balls in their briefcase, or else they just leave them in their desk drawer and only put them on at the office. Hot Chicks do not date men with *BMS*.

Butt Class: You may not believe us, but we used to have a lame, flat, white-girl ass until we got that flat ass to the gym and started taking lots of butt classes! Butt classes are also called boring things like Body Sculpting or Weight Training, but we think our term is more descriptive. Anyway, just like the Build a Bear Workshop that they have now, this is like a Build a Butt Workshop. (We also hold a Build a Boyfriend Workshop, but we'll talk about that in the next book.) Butt classes include tons of squats, dead lifts and lunges, and we prescribe taking them twice a week for maximum butt benefits.

Everybody Wants to be Italian: Coming Soon! Shameless Plug!

Fantasy Sequence: A daydream that you purposely create, or one that just sort of happens when something or someone is in the back of your mind - your imagination runs wild and creates something totally fun. For example, you my have *fantasy sequences* about finally telling off that annoying chick at work who reads your emails over your shoulder, making out with your boyfriend in the middle of a boring meeting, or maybe just looking absolutely adorable and irresistible as you flirt with the hot barista at Starbucks.

Fucked Up: We hope that you can tell when something in your life is fucked up, but we are referring here to when your FOOD is fucked up. Fucked up food includes anything that is bad for you, high in calories and/or fat or is just downright strange. For instance, a salad can be healthy but fucked up because of too many weird components, or Chinese Food can be fucked up because it is secretly covered in corn syrup that will make you feel puffy and disgusting.

Heyday: The very best, most magical, hottest time of your life - no matter what age box you check, or if you're married, single, gay or straight. Your *heyday* begins when you stop having a pity party and decide that you're hot and worth all the fun in the world. You will look back one day and shake your head and giggle, remembering all of the fun, crazy, ridiculous times you had during your *heyday.* And it will be worth it.

Heydayish: Our code word for when we're in the mood for some loving. Hot Chicks don't use the word horny, and there aren't many other good options to describe this feeling, either.

We're feeling *heydayish* when we really, really want a big giant boy to go downtown and then bake in our bed. Examples for using it in a sentence: "*I only went home with him because I've been feeling heydayish.*" Or, "*I'm not going out tonight because I am feeling heydayish, and I might do something stupid.*"

LSE: Stands for *Low Self Esteem.* It is a disease that infects everyone from time to time, but Hot Chicks try really hard to cure themselves of this plague. The best thing about the term LSE is that it can be used as a noun, verb, adjective, or whatever. For example, you can be *feeling LSE,* someone can just *be LSE,* or your *LSE* can just act up unexpectedly. *LSE* is NOT hot, ladies, and recovering from this deadly infection is the first and biggest step to truly being a Hot Chick.

Magic: This is our word for something or someone that is perfectly hot, perfectly fun, or makes you feel like the happiest girl on the planet. Example for using it in a sentence: "*I'm wearing my magic pants tonight,*" "*Was your date magic?*" or, "*Something happened, our trip was magical!*"

Mary Kate: We don't mean to seem insensitive, but we started using this term for being a little bit anorexic or just fucked up about food. It is not hot to be *Mary Kate,* but this term can be used in many forms, which we love. Examples in a sentence are, "*You only ate two bites of your dinner - are you pulling a Mary Kate?*" or "*Did you see how grossly skinny that girl was? She's totally Mary Kate.*"

OWL Syndrome: Stands for *Overwhelmed With Life. OWL Syndrome* can occur when you have way too much going on all at once, or if something unexpected happens (whether it's good or bad) that totally freaks you out. Example*: OWL Syndrome* can take effect when your boss puts a giant folder on your desk filled with crap she wants you to finish by 6 p.m., you get a nasty passive-aggressive e-mail from your mother, and then that cute guy you met online calls to say he wants to have dinner with you tonight at 7.

Play Small: The origins of this term are actually from a Nelson Mandela quote - *"Your playing small does not serve the world. There's nothing enlightening about shrinking so that others feel secure around you."* We couldn't have said it better ourselves. Hot Chicks do not *play small,* apologize for who we are, or act LSE* to make people feel better about themselves. That's not hot, and to stop *playing small* is a big step in living like a Hot Chick.

Red Flags: These are warning signs - sometimes they are giant and sometimes they're very subtle. Examples: A guy you're dating says to you, *"I would tell you that you're beautiful, but I'm sure you hear that all the time."* A little *red flag* should go up. This guy probably has BMS*. Or how about when a superior in your business invites you to coffee to talk about future projects, and then "coffee" mysteriously turns into a candlelight dinner where he orders beef Carpaccio, a bottle of expensive vino, and buys you a rose. A

GIANT *red flag* should go up, telling you that he doesn't want you involved in his business plan; he wants you naked in his bed.

Self-Destructive Fantasy Sequences: These are the negative, nasty versions of *fantasy sequences**. This is when your mind latches onto something horrific and upsetting and your imagination runs wild with it. *Self-destructive fantasy sequences* are usually brought on by fears or a giant case of *LSE**. Example: If your ex-husband was a pathological liar and was living a double life with another woman, then it's highly possible that you might have *self-destructive fantasy sequences* about your new boyfriend cheating on you. You might picture your new love getting a blowjob in the bathroom at his office, or imagine him sending dirty e-mails to every woman in his contact list. It is not hot to indulge in these obnoxious thoughts! Don't let *self destructive fantasy sequences* happen. You are only wasting precious time and energy that could be used towards your *heyday**.

Twitterpated: To be giddy and so overjoyed and anxious with feelings of love that it makes your heart pop out of your eyes whenever you're around you new crush. Origins - Disney's *Bambi*, when all the little animals were mating and falling in love because it was spring. Examples for using it in a sentence: *"I know he's the one because it's been a year and a half and I'm still twitterpated,"* or, *"I really didn't mean to have sex with him on the first date, but I couldn't help it, I was so twitterpated!"*

Universe: The *universe* is a stand-in for God or fate or whatever you believe in. The Hot Chicks believe firmly that the *universe* loves us and takes care of us and gives us exactly what we need in its proper time. But we have a give and take relationship with the *universe* - we have to tell it what we want and prepare ourselves so that we're ready when we get it. It's also important not to put bad things out into the *universe.* Examples in a sentence: *"I keep getting hit on by creepy guys - I must be sending out a weird vibe and confusing the universe,"* or *"I feel good about that job interview. I did my best, and now it's up to the universe."*

Acknowledgments!

From Both Of Us:

We know how easy it is to look totally obnoxious and self-important in acknowledgments, so we will try our best to avoid that. But we have to thank these people: First, our agent, Dan Mandel (a.k.a. Agent Dan), who has believed in this project from the very beginning and through all sorts of incarnations. Dan, your support has meant the world to us! Courtney Chesla casually referred to her "heyday," which really woke us up and in many ways actually changed our lives, so thank you Courtney. Kathleen Tomasik (now Black!) was the first to introduce us to the dire affliction of LSE. Thank you, Kathleen, for helping us cure ourselves and for inspiring us. Justin Heimberg has allowed us to pick his brain relentlessly, which has proved extremely helpful. David Brown is a publicity genius, and more importantly has very nice eyes. David, you're the best! Paolo Pepe helped us find our lovely designer, and Julienne Park made our book quite possibly look even prettier on the outside than it is inside! Thank you so much, Julienne. And an extra big thanks to all of you Hot Chicks out there who picked up this book! You inspire us more than anything on the planet.

Personal Acknowledgments!

From Jodi:

Thank you to my beautiful mom for believing in this book and in me as a writer more than anyone, and for being the first Hot Chick to really prove that this stuff works! Your support of me and this book has meant so much to me. Dad, thanks for giving me your sense of humor (most importantly!), for giving me the confidence to do whatever I want, and for always being there for me. I am so grateful to have you both, and thank you to the rest of my family for believing in me, too. I am lucky enough to count three of the funniest men on the planet as my friends - Darren Belitsky, Jeff Sank and Adam Szymkowicz - all of you at one point or another gave me brilliant notes, let me steal your jokes, and/or told me that I was hilarious. Thanks, guys! I honestly can't even begin to thank my brilliant and truly beautiful writing partner, who not only magically made me into a better person, but is also one of the smartest, funniest and kindest women on the planet. Cerina, there is no one I would rather be in business with! And certainly not least, thank you Dan for every single thing you do, for drinking coffee (now you're perfect!), for never sneaking too much butter into my eggs, and for making me feel hot every day.

From Cerina:

First, thank you Mommy for setting a perfect example of what a Hot Chick should be. If you looked up "amazing" in the dictionary, a picture of your beautiful face would be there, and your faith in me is what keeps me going. And Dad, thank you for making me feel like a princess, teaching me how to follow my dreams, and for making me do every sport as a kid even though I sucked. It taught me to push myself beyond what I think I can do. Thank you Gino and Angela for loving me and never judging me. Thank you Adam Seid for believing that I'm a "star" (even when I don't eat like a Hot Chick), and being the best manager that exists in this crazy business. Libby, thank you for giving me a crash course in not "playing small." I have to give a shout-out to my huge Italian family for always making food a celebration. And to my little Jodi-face, the best business partner ever! Words can not express how much I cherish your friendship. I feel so blessed to have your beauty, brains, grace, humor, honesty and understanding in my life...you changed my life. And to my darling Benj, thank you for making me believe in love at first sight, for the M&M pancakes, and always making me feel beautiful. Your love inspires me.